WORLD WAR II
THE START OF WORLD WAR II: THE FLOOD OF THE GERMAN TIDE

WORLD WAR II
THE START OF WORLD WAR II: THE FLOOD OF THE GERMAN TIDE

MASON CREST

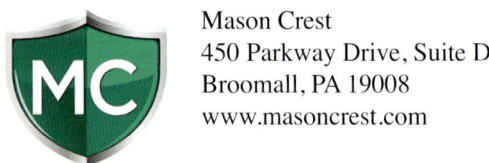

Mason Crest
450 Parkway Drive, Suite D
Broomall, PA 19008
www.masoncrest.com

© 2018 by Mason Crest, an imprint of National Highlights, Inc.

All rights reserved. No part of this publication may be reproduced or transmitted in any form or by any means, electronic or mechanical, including photocopying, recording, taping, or any information storage and retrieval system, without permission in writing from the copyright holder.

Cataloging-in-Publication Data on file with the Library of Congress.

Printed and bound in the United States of America.

First printing
9 8 7 6 5 4 3 2 1

ISBN: 978-1-4222-3894-3
Series ISBN: 978-1-4222-3893-6
ebook ISBN: 978-1-4222-7904-5
ebook series ISBN: 978-1-4222-7903-8

Produced by Regency House Publishing Limited
The Manor House
High Street
Buntingford
Hertfordshire
SG9 9AB
United Kingdom

www.regencyhousepublishing.com

Text copyright © 2018 Regency House Publishing Limited/Christopher Chant.

PAGE 2: *Troops from the United Kingdom enter Germany.*

PAGE 3: *Light tanks from the United Kingdom.*

RIGHT: *A U.S. soldier offers a French child some chocolate.*

PAGE 6: *Heinz Guderian in his special command vehicle, equipped with maps, radio equipment, and (bottom left) an Enigma cipher machine.*

TITLES IN THE WORLD WAR II SERIES:

The Start of World War II: The Flood of the German Tide
The Allied Powers Fight Back
Japanese Aggression in the Pacific
The Defeat of the Nazis: The Allied Victory in Europe
The End of World War II: The Japanese Surrender

CONTENTS

National World War II Memorial 10

Chapter One
The Defeat of Poland 12

Chapter Two
The Scandinavian Conflicts 18

Chapter Three
Germany Strikes to the West and The Battle of Britain 28

Chapter Four
The Naval War 1939 –1940 40

Chapter Five
The War in Africa 44

Chapter Six
Germany Takes Yugoslavia and Greece 54

Chapter Seven
Operation Barbarossa: The German Invasion of the USSR 60

Chapter Eight
The Battle of the Atlantic 1940–1941 68

Time Line of World War II 72

Series Glossary of Key Terms 74

Further Reading and Internet Resources 75

Index 76

Further Information 80

KEY ICONS TO LOOK FOR:

Words to Understand: These words with their easy-to-understand definitions will increase the reader's understanding of the text, while building vocabulary skills.

Sidebars: This boxed material within the main text allows readers to build knowledge, gain insights, explore possibilities, and broaden their perspectives by weaving together additional information to provide realistic and holistic perspectives.

Educational Videos: Readers can view videos by scanning our QR codes, providing them with additional content to supplement the text. Examples include news coverage, moments in history, speeches, iconic sports moments, and much more!

Text-Dependent Questions: These questions send the reader back to the text for more careful attention to the evidence presented here.

Research Projects: Readers are pointed toward areas of further inquiry connected to each chapter. Suggestions are provided for projects that encourage deeper research and analysis.

Series Glossary of Key Terms: This back-of-the-book glossary contains terminology used throughout the series. Words found here increase the reader's ability to read and comprehend high-level books and articles in this field.

OPPOSITE: *Finnish troops on skis. All soldiers are trained in ski combat, and skiing is a part of standard required training for conscripts.*

National World War II Memorial

The National World War II Memorial in Washington, D.C., is dedicated to the 16 million people who served in the American armed forces during World War II. The memorial also honors the 400,000 who gave the ultimate sacrifice for their country. Those who supported the war effort at home are honored too. The memorial symbolizes World War II as the defining event of the 20th century.

The memorial is situated on a 7.4-acre (3-hectare) site. It was created by designer and architect Friedrich St. Florian who won a national open competition for its design. The construction of memorial took place between 2001 and 2004 and then opened to the public on April 29, 2004; its official dedication took place a month later, on May 29. It was commission by President Clinton in 1993 who authorized the American Battle Monuments Commission (ABMC) to establish a World War II memorial in the Washington, D.C. area.

The memorial is an elliptical shaped plaza built around a splendid fountain and pool, with water jets in its center. Built in a semi-classical style, there are 56 granite columns forming a semi-circle around the perimeter. Each one is designed to symbolize the unity of the states, federal territories, and District of Columbia. The entry walkway is flanked by ornate balustrades decorated with 24 bronze bas-reliefs.

At the mid point of the plaza there are two pavillions decorated with bronzes, featuring Baldachins, American Eagles, and World War II Victory Medals. The pavillions represent the Atlantic and Pacific theaters.

At the western end of the memorial is a curved Freedom Wall bearing a field of 4,048 golden stars, each of which stands for 100 American military deaths in the war. Before it lies a granite curb inscribed "Here we mark the price of freedom."

Throughout the memorial are inscribed quotations from eminent military and political figures, including Gen. (later Pres.) Dwight D. Eisenhower, U.S. Presidents Franklin D. Roosevelt and Harry S. Truman, Col. Oveta Culp Hobby, Adm. Chester W. Nimitz, Gen. George C. Marshall, and Gen. Douglas MacArthur.

The National World War II Memorial is located at the east end of the Reflecting Pool on the Mall, opposite the Lincoln Memorial and west of the Washington Monument. The memorial is maintained by the U.S. National Park Service, and receives almost 5 million visitors each year. It is open 24 hours a day and is free to all visitors.

WORLD WAR II
Chapter One
THE DEFEAT OF POLAND

The **Nazi** party came to power in Germany in January 1933 with the intention of tearing up the Treaty of Versailles, signed in 1919 to end Germany's part in World War I and which had drastically curtailed the size of Germany's armed forces. Only thus, the Nazis under Adolf Hitler believed, would Germany be restored to its "rightful" place as the most powerful nation in Europe, with all people of German blood living in areas outside the Reich properly incorporated into the new and larger "Greater Germany." The treaty had limited the German forces to a 100,000-man army with no armor, a small navy, and no air force. But under the leadership of General Hans von Seeckt, the army had been rebuilt during the 1920s as a highly trained, professional core on which a much larger force could be based as soon as conscription was once again possible. Development of armor and warplanes proceeded under various guises, much of it at training areas which the USSR granted in exchange for technical information, and civilian flying schools were used to build a large pool of trained pilots. In the spring of 1935 Hitler announced that Germany was repudiating the Treaty of Versailles, that the country now had an air force, and

> **Words to Understand**
>
> **Luftwaffe:** The German word for air force.
>
> **Nazi:** A member of a German fascist party under Adolf Hitler.
>
> **Rhineland:** Part of Germany west of the Rhine river.

that conscription would be introduced to bring its army up to a strength of 300,000 men.

The UK and France made no effective protest, which served to convince Hitler that these moribund nations had lost the will to act decisively. In March 1936 Hitler openly proved this by reoccupying the **Rhineland**, against the advice of his generals, who knew that the army was still poorly trained, lacked modern equipment, and was far smaller than that of France.

In March 1938, with the apparent approval of the bulk of its population, Austria was annexed to the Reich. Once again, the UK and France made no effort to prevent this from happening. Despite

warnings, the British and French governments were determined to avoid war, preferring to give way to Hitler rather than run any risks. But in the fall of 1938 the Führer (leader) made his first overt move against an independent state when he demanded that the Sudetenland, the western border region of Czechoslovakia, with its 3 million Germans, should be annexed to the Reich on the grounds that its inhabitants were being maltreated by the native population.

The Start of World War II: The Flood of the German Tide

Czechoslovakia was a model democracy, prosperous, and socially advanced, with large and well equipped armed forces in defenses which would have proved difficult for the Germans to attack. The government prepared to resist but, as Hitler had foreseen, under pressure from the UK and France an "honorable" solution was found to guarantee "peace in our time:" the Sudetenland, with all of the Czech frontier defenses, was handed over to Germany. Hitler had removed a potentially difficult threat on his southern flank and was further convinced that he had nothing to fear from the UK and France. He completed the occupation of Czechoslovakia in March 1939, which now meant that the western democracies could no longer close their eyes to the true nature of Hitler's plans and accelerated the pace of their rearmament. But it would take many years to redress the long period of

OPPOSITE LEFT: *The Polish artillery arm was indifferently equipped and, for the most part, comprised light horse-drawn rather than mechanically-towed medium and heavy equipment.*

OPPOSITE RIGHT: *A Polish soldier, accompanied by a militiaman and a civilian, examine the wreckage of a German warplane. The German air force suffered heavier casualties, often from ground fire, than had been estimated, but proved very effective in the provision of tactical support for the grounds forces.*

ABOVE: *Polish troops in training before the outbreak of World War II. The bulk of the Polish army was located well forward against the Polish-German frontier and, once the German spearheads had broken through to link up in their rear areas, most formations were trapped and eventually forced to surrender.*

RIGHT: *German troops examine destroyed Polish armour. The Polish armored forces were small, lacked any modern tactical doctrine, and were only very indifferently equipped. These are Renault FT-17 light tanks – two-man French vehicles dating from the period of World War I.*

their military retrenchment and inactivity, the German forces being now more than equal in strength to their potential opponents.

Hitler was ready to turn on Poland as his next victim. Here the Danzig "corridor," providing Poland with access to the Baltic Sea but at the same time separating East Prussia from the rest of the Reich, presented Hitler with the excuse for intervention.

Regardless of the non-aggression treaty between Poland and Germany, Adolf Hitler insisted on the provision of greater *Lebensraum* (living space) for the German people. Detailed planning of the

The Defeat of Poland

campaign to take Poland started in April 1939, and on August 23 the signature of a Russo-German non-aggression pact freed Germany from the threat of any Soviet intervention against the German forces, and established a demarcation line for the future partition of Poland after Germany and the USSR had invaded respectively from the west and the east.

One of Hitler's main concerns was to delay the UK's mobilization for as long as possible, particularly as the UK had once more reiterated its pledge to assist Poland should the latter be invaded. To this end, Hitler maintained a show of sham diplomacy to convince the world of his peaceful intent. He even postponed the start of the offensive and continued his diplomatic appearances to make sure that Poland's potential allies would be ill-prepared at the time of the German invasion. By the end of August Hitler could wait no longer, and on September 1, 1939 the invasion was launched, and with it World War II as the UK and France responded to Germany's refusal to withdraw by declaring war two days later.

Poland could not easily be defended as it was open to attack on three sides: from East Prussia, Pomerania, and Slovakia. The Polish frontier contained a

huge westward salient stretching 1,250 miles (2010km) from the Soviet-Lithuanian border to the Carpathian Mountains, excluding the defense requirements of the Danzig corridor linking the Polish port of Danzig with the rest of Poland. The French had advised the Poles to base their defense along the line of the Niemen, Bobr,

Narew, Vistula, and San rivers, and therefore behind a strong river barrier along a front of only 420 miles (675km). The Poles were unwilling to give up the industrial and agricultural regions to the west of this line, but could not defend 1,250 miles effectively; Marshal Edward Rydz-Smigly, Poland's commander-in-chief, exacerbated matters by deploying many of his troops in Danzig and around Poznan, although he had received accurate intelligence reports on the forces massing against him. On September 1, this huge front was defended by only 17 divisions, three infantry brigades, and six cavalry brigades. There was no adequate command structure between Rydz-Smigly and the commanders of the Pomeranian, Modlin, Poznan, Lódz, Krakow, Carpathian, Prussian, and Narew Armies. There were also the Pyskor and the Wyskow Groups in reserve, the former including Poland's only tank unit, the Warsaw Armored Brigade. The Polish air force had only 433 operational aircraft, the majority of them now obsolete and including the PZL P.7 and P.11 fighters and the PZL P.23 bomber.

Hitler's objective was the swift destruction of the Polish armed forces. Converging attacks on Warsaw would be

The Start of World War II: The Flood of the German Tide

OPPOSITE ABOVE: *Polish weapons gathered by the Germans in the aftermath of their destruction of the Polish army in September 1939.*

OPPOSITE BELOW: *Captured Polish troops march off into captivity, to be used as forced labor under the harshest of conditions and with little food or clothing. Vast numbers of Poles were lost in this way between 1939 and 1945.*

ABOVE: *Heinz Guderian (center), seen here with Adolf Hitler, was an architect of the German armored establishment, and one of the key commanders in the German defeat of Poland in 1939.*

RIGHT: *Photographed while speaking with Hitler and other leading German officials, Karl Rudolf Gerd von Rundstedt was a German officer of the old school, who felt nothing but disdain for the Nazis but regarded it as his duty to fight for his country. An officer of very senior rank throughout the war, Gerd von Rundstedt was a skilled army group and theater commander, and was the leader of Army Group South in the Polish campaign.*

launched from Silesia, Pomerania, and East Prussia, and the German forces would execute two pincer movements, one on Warsaw and another farther to the east with the task of trapping Polish forces retreating in that direction. The German army had 13 armored and motorized divisions in the vanguard of the offensive, and 31 infantry divisions. The forces were deployed in two main army groups. Army Group North, commanded by Colonel-General Fedor von Bock, comprised on its left flank the 3rd Army under General Georg von Küchler, and on its right flank the 4th Army under General Günther-Hans von Kluge. Army Group North would attack from East Prussia and Pomerania, its left flank taking on the Polish forces in the corridor and then driving south toward Warsaw, while its right would attack from Pomerania and defeat any Polish troops guarding the corridor. Army Group South, commanded by Colonel-General Gerd von Rundstedt, had on its left wing the 8th Army under General Johannes Blaskowitz, on its right wing the 14th Army under General Wilhelm List, and in its center the 10th Army under General Walther von Reichenau, its task being to attack from Silesia and Slovakia. The 8th Army would engage Polish forces in the region of Poznan-Kutno, the 10th Army would drive north-east toward Lódz and on to Warsaw, and the 14th Army would strike across the Carpathians, pinning down the Poles around Krakow and Przemysl.

Each army group was supported by an air fleet: Luftflotte 1, commanded by General Albert Kesselring, would operate with Army Group North, and Luftflotte 4, commanded by General Alexander Löhr, would support Army Group South. The two air fleets had 897 bombers, dive-bombers, and ground-attack aircraft, 210 fighters and 474 reconnaissance and transport machines.

Poland did not begin its general mobilization until 11.00am on August 31 and was thus caught with 13 of its 40 divisions still moving toward their concentration points, while a further nine were not yet mobilized when the Germans attacked. Ahead of the armies, the Luftwaffe prepared the way, its mission being to destroy the Polish air force on the ground, then to assist the German ground forces, attack military installations and communications, and terrorize the civilian population. Despite a gallant resistance, the Polish air force was effectively destroyed by the third day, although Polish pilots maintained sporadic attacks until September 17, operating with great determination and skill. The Luftwaffe, however, reigned

The Defeat of Poland

The German Tank
Though Western propaganda portrayed the German army as a armored juggernaut, crushing beneath the treads of its tanks all that the Junkers Ju 87 Stuka dive-bombers had not already destroyed, the German Panzer arm was in reality troubled by the mix of its tanks, their modest capability, and their comparatively poor reliability. Where the Germans did have a decisive advantage, however, was in the concentration of their armor in dedicated Panzer divisions, used in full accord with carefully prepared tactical and operational doctrines.

German offensive. Rydz-Smigly ordered his forces to withdraw eastward on September 6, but this was already too late to save the frontier armies. The German 10th Army rapidly approached Warsaw, and though its two Panzer divisions had reached the city they failed to take it on September 8 for lack of infantry support. The rest of the 10th Army reached the Vistula two days later and defeated the Lódz Army, while farther to the north, the German 4th Army reached and crossed the Vistula and began its march on Warsaw.

The Pomeranian and Poznan Armies, falling back on Warsaw, met the German 8th Army, which attempted to block its retreat north of Lódz. Although virtually surrounded by Germans, the commander of the Poznan Army, General Kutrzeba, resolved to strike south against the flank of the main German advance to the east. This courageous move resulted in the Battle of the Bzura, in which the Poles succeeded in capturing bridgeheads across the Bzura river near Lowicz and driving back the German 30th Division. This crisis drew into the battle Panzer and motorized corps, and even a corps from the 4th Army in the north. These reinforcements, and the persistent Stuka

supreme. Its Junkers Ju 87 Stuka dive-bomber units delivered pinpoint attacks at crucial moments and locations, the German ability to coordinate air and ground forces representing a new feature in warfare, giving great flexibility to fast-moving armored and motorized formations lacking the support of traditional artillery unable to keep pace with them.

Within a week the German forces had advanced deep into Poland, their armored units pushing on ahead of the infantry. If the German equipment was modern, so were the tactics, and generals such as Guderian, Höpner, Hoth, von Kleist, and von Wietersheim quickly displayed their skill in command of the Panzer divisions. Against them, the Poles, having only one armored brigade, could do little, and the Polish armies on the frontiers were quickly driven back by the

The Start of World War II: The Flood of the German Tide

OPPOSITE: German infantrymen wait in the lee of a tank for the order to move forward against their next objective.

ABOVE: German troops prepare to cross the German-Polish frontier, in this case against no discernible opposition.

RIGHT: Conquered Poland became the fiefdom of Hans Frank, a brutal man who was finally condemned for his crimes by the Nuremberg war trials tribunal and hanged in 1946.

attacks, forced the 170,000 Poles to surrender after a hard fight at Lowicz on September 19.

To the south the German 14th Army had driven on and reached the San river. Meanwhile, the inner pincers were closing around Warsaw as the 3rd Army encircled the city from the east and the 8th Army from the west. At the same time, a start was made on the outer pincer movement as the 3rd Army's left-hand column struck out for Brest-Litovsk, 100 miles (160km) behind the front. General Heinz Guderian, who had enjoyed great success earlier in the campaign in the Danzig area with XIX Panzer Corps, was instrumental in the second pincer movement. On September 9 the Panzers crossed the Narew river upstream of Lomza, reaching Brest-Litovsk on September 15, the 3rd Panzer Division pressing ahead to make contact with leading elements of the 10th and 14th Armies approaching from the south. The 14th Army had reached Lvov in the east before wheeling north to meet General Guderian. The pincers met and snapped shut, trapping thousands with no hope of escape.

The Soviets were surprised at the speed of the German advance, and on September 17 announced that Poland and its government had now ceased to exist and that the USSR must intervene to protect their own sphere of interest, namely the portion of Poland east of the Narew, Vistula, and San rivers. The Soviet armies swarmed across the virtually undefended eastern frontier of Poland, ending any further hopes the Poles may have had of resisting. The Soviet columns rolled west on a broad front, and on September 18 occupied Vilna, meeting the Germans at Brest-Litovsk. The ruin and subjugation of Poland was nearly complete; on September 18 the Polish government fled to Romania, while Warsaw and Modlin were still holding out against the Germans. Warsaw, which was being violently bombarded daily by air and heavy artillery, surrendered on September 27, while Modlin held out valiantly for a further day.

Thus in less than one month the nation of Poland, with its 35 million people, was eliminated from the map. The geographical area was divided into two by the Treaty of Delimitation and Friendship, signed on September 28 by Germany and the USSR. In central Poland, the demarcation line connected the Bug and Vistula rivers, and was marked by the San river in Galicia. Lithuania was incorporated into the Soviet sphere in return for German sovereignty over parts of the province of Warsaw and the whole of Lublin. Poland had lost 694,000 prisoners to Germany and 217,000 to the USSR, but 100,000 Poles had been able to make their escape to the west by way of Romania.

WORLD WAR II

Chapter Two
THE SCANDINAVIAN CONFLICTS

THE WINTER WAR
Finland, with a population of only some 4.5 million spread over 130,000 square miles (336700km²), was now the location of one of the most amazing conflicts in history, in which Finland's tiny army was able to hold out against the might of the USSR and, at the beginning of a campaign that lasted 105 days, inflict severe casualties on the aggressor. A Russo-Finnish Non-Aggression Pact had been signed in 1934, but on October 14, 1939 the Soviet leader, Iosef Stalin, began to make various territorial demands on Finland in return for a considerable border adjustment in Karelia. Finland, wishing to retain its neutrality, offered to compromise on these demands, but the USSR would brook no interference with its plan. The Soviet forces were already prepared for the offensive, having reconnoitred the Karelian isthmus and Finland's ports, roads, industrial areas, and fortifications from the air, and reached the conclusion that the Finns were hopelessly ill-equipped to defend themselves.

On November 30, without any formal declaration of war, the Soviet land, sea, and air onslaught began, with Helsinki bombed heavily right from the start. The Finns had begun calling up their reserves, but when the Soviet offensive started the commander in chief, Marshal Carl Gustaf von Mannerheim, had only nine divisions at his disposal. The II and III Corps were deployed in the Karelian isthmus with five divisions under Lieutenant-General Hugo Ostermann; the IV Corps was on the east shore of Lake Ladoga with two divisions under Major-General J. Woldemar Hagglund; the Central Finland Group comprised the V Corps of nine frontier battalions under Major-General Vilpo Tuompo; the Lapland Group with four independent battalions commanded by Major-General Kurt Wallenius; while two incomplete divisions (I Corps) and a cavalry brigade formed the reserve. Facing these limited Finnish forces, the Soviets had in the Karelian isthmus the 7th Army with eight divisions, a tank corps and two independent tank brigades to force the Mannerheim Line, take Viipuri, and push on to Helsinki; on the east shore of Lake Ladoga the 8th Army with six divisions was to assist the 7th

ABOVE LEFT: In the winter warfare of 1939–40, better trained and better equipped Finnish troops, fighting on home ground and fully acclimatized to the harsh conditions, were able to perform far better than their Soviet opponents.

ABOVE: A useful extemporized weapon, favored by the Finns, was the "Molotov cocktail," a bottle filled with petrol and other flammables that would break on hitting a tank, with the spilt contents then catching fire.

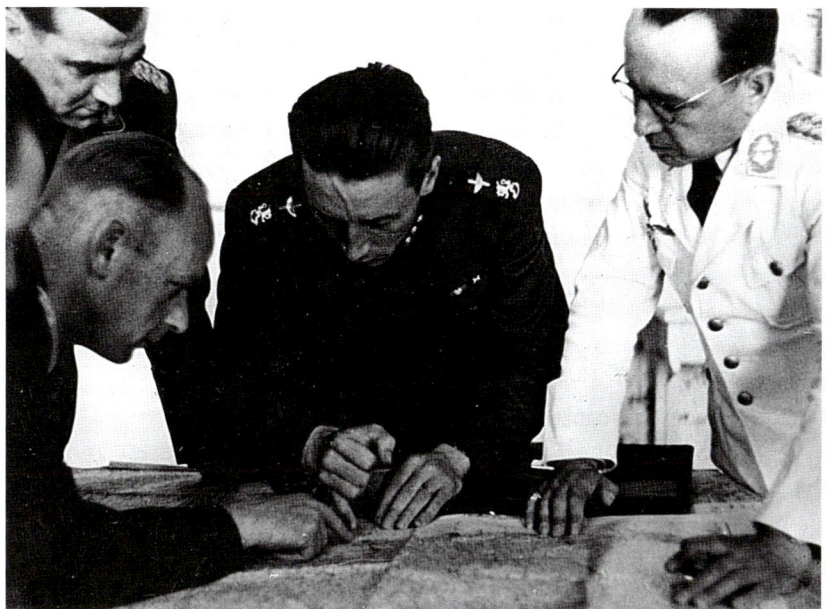

tactics and military manuals, and was thus able to predict Soviet thinking, which was tied rigidly to set formulae. In the event, manuals were useless in the winter conditions of Finland, where the

ABOVE LEFT: *German and Finnish military liaison team assesses the tactical situation.*

LEFT: *A German 1.5-in (37-mm) anti-aircraft gun, in use on the coast of the Gulf of Finland. In 1939–40 the Germans did not provide much material support for the Finns as a result of their Non-Aggression Pact with the Soviets of August 1939.*

ABOVE: *The Finnish commander in chief was Marshal Carl Gustaf von Mannerheim, an ex-Tsarist officer and an expert in defensive warfare.*

Army by drawing off the Finnish defense; farther north the 9th Army with four divisions was to launch two columns, the more southerly to make for Oulu and the more northerly for Kemi in central Finland; and in Lapland the 14th Army with two divisions was to take Petsamo and sever Finnish links with Norway.

Mannerheim knew there were good lines of communication only in the center of Finland and that the Finns must prevent the Soviets from reaching them. He was familiar with Soviet

The Scandinavian Conflicts

The Winter War Between Finland and Russia

Soviets immediately succumbed to the cruel weather, while heavy snow blocked their advance and grounded their aircraft. On the other hand, the Finns proved themselves masters of irregular warfare, striking hard in the dark or during snowstorms, or appearing without warning on skis, dressed in white, to attack and disappear; in fact, to the Soviet forces the Finns seemed to be everywhere. Many booby-trap devices were used to slow the invaders, minefields guarded all approaches, and the Finns were expert at destroying tanks with "Molotov cocktails" – bottles filled with a mixture of crude kerosene, tar, and petrol. Mannerheim's reservists mostly wore their own clothes, perhaps with an identifying cap or belt, but no matter how indifferent they appeared by more conventional military standards, the Finnish soldiers were perfectly suited to the conditions.

The Finns were amazed as masses of heavy tanks bore down on them, but the Soviets seemed uncertain as to how they could use their matériel superiority to the greatest effect, and the tanks became trapped in the snow. The Soviet troops were inexperienced and uncoordinated, also lacking in winter warfare training, while Stalin's purges of 1937–38 had robbed them of many of their best leaders. At first the Soviet soldiers bore up well, but as the temperature continued to plummet their morale began to flag. Their weapons froze, and many thousands of them died from the cold. The Finns were better clothed and knew how to keep their weapons serviceable in such conditions; they also had the advantage of fighting in territory with which they were familiar.

The Soviets were checked on almost all fronts. They did manage to take Petsamo, in the far north, in the middle of December by overwhelming the small Finnish defense with the superior firepower of a large force based on Murmansk. In the south, however, on the Karelian isthmus, that separated Lake Ladoga from the Gulf of Finland, the Mannerheim Line comprised 90 miles (145km) of anti-tank obstacles, field fortifications, ditches and trenches, which stopped the Soviets as they tried to break though a line of which they know virtually nothing. The fighting was almost continuous, with the Soviets constantly committing fresh divisions and constantly being beaten off. The Soviet 7th Army's 139th and 75th Divisions reached Tolvajärvi on December 12, but here their 45,000 men, 335 pieces of artillery and 140 tanks were ambushed and annihilated by seven Finnish battalions under Major-General Paavo Talvela's group with 9,000 men and 20 pieces of artillery.

In central Finland, the column of the Soviet 9th Army was counterattacked at Suomussalmi on its intended advance to the port of Oulu on the Gulf of Bothnia which, if successful, would have cut Finland in two. Major-General Hjalmar Siilasvuo led the Finns in this furious battle; the Soviet 163rd Division was cut off after a Finnish attack lasting 17 days, while the Soviet 44th Division was destroyed as it also tried to retreat. Some 800 men of the 44th Division dug in and the Finns attacked them at will, at the same time capturing an assortment of their weapons.

There emerged a pattern of attack and counterattack on all fronts, and both sides rapidly became exhausted. The Finns pushed the Soviets back toward the USSR, by which time the Soviets had lost approximately 27,500 dead. Stalin was furious, and on December 12 the League of Nations condemned the Soviet aggression in Finland. Hitler remained neutral and refused to allow Italian aid to Finland to pass through Germany. The USSR, therefore, determined to beat the Finns at all costs, committed some 45 divisions, or 40 percent of the Soviet land forces of European USSR. Stalin also changed the senior leadership of the forces on the Finnish front, with Marshal Semyon Timoshenko assuming overall command. Timoshenko's primary task was to create a breakthrough on the Karelian front, but after failing to penetrate the Mannerheim Line, the Soviet 7th Army was shifted to the Gulf of Finland, the 13th Army taking its place with its right flank on Lake Ladoga. Timoshenko's forces totaled 24 infantry divisions with three more in reserve, backed by 20 regiments of artillery and seven armored brigades, all supported by 450 aircraft.

Mannerheim rightly predicted the Soviets would attack east of Summa village, in the west of the Karelian isthmus, where the open fields would allow the Soviets to concentrate armor and infantry. The offensive began on February 1, 1940 in bitterly cold conditions. The Soviets had learned vital lessons since November, and were now

better coordinated, often directed from observation balloons. They used trains of armored sledges drawn by tanks to move infantry, and employed flamethrower tanks. Heavy artillery deluged the Finns, steadily wearing them down, and the widespread bombing of the Finnish rear areas marked the beginning of the end. The Soviets attacked in massive waves, and despite huge losses to the Finnish artillery, machine gun, and rifle fire, finally began to make progress. On February 6 the final assault began when three divisions with 150 tanks attacked along a 5-mile (8-km) line with the support of 200 aircraft. On February 7, the Soviet forces penetrated the region of Muolaa, striking at Summa. Timoshenko then shifted the weight of the offensive farther to the east, and by February 11 the Soviets had broken through the Mannerheim Line. The Finns withdrew in good order, counter-attacking all the while, and took up a new defensive, which, being longer than the Mannerheim Line, stretched their resources. The Finns nonetheless continued to harass the Soviet forces, the Soviet losses averaging 800 men and between 10 and 20 tanks per day during February 20–22.

On February 24 the Soviets seized Koivisto island, in the frozen Gulf of Finland, the 7th Army having been instructed to cross the ice to take Viipuri on the mainland. Soon after, the main road linking Viipuri to Helsinki was taken by the Soviets. The Finns had by this time lost 25,000 men killed and 43,000 wounded, and were physically and morally exhausted. Continued resistance

OPPOSITE: *The fight against Soviet aggression was a national effort, as represented here by Finnish women serving as auxiliaries to spot and report the numbers and course of approaching Soviet warplanes.*

OPPOSITE RIGHT: *The Soviets made extensive use of armored vehicles, but suffered huge losses to mines, artillery, and dedicated antitank teams armed with antitank grenades and "Molotov cocktails."*

seemed impossible because there was no more manpower and ammunition available. Mannerheim, therefore, felt that it was time to find a solution which would end the fighting. On March 12, 1940 the Russo-Finnish Treaty was signed, ceding 16,000sq miles (41440km²) of Finland to the USSR, leaving the Finns with a frontier which left them effectively naked to further Soviet aggression and giving the Soviets almost the whole of Karelia. But the Soviet losses had also been enormous, with something in the order of 200,000 dead and 400,000 wounded.

THE GERMAN SEIZURE OF DENMARK & NORWAY

On December 14, 1939 Vidkun Quisling, the leader of the small Norwegian fascist party, the Party of National Union, alleged that British intervention in Scandinavia was imminent. Hitler immediately ordered preliminary studies for a possible expedition to Norway, with Denmark as a possible stepping stone in the process. At this time Germany was obtaining two-thirds of its high-grade iron ore from northern Sweden via the ports of Luleå in Sweden and Narvik in Norway. If the Allies were to cut these

supply lines, Germany's war-making industries would be hard hit. Various means of achieving this were considered, including the mining of the Leads, the sea corridor between the mainland and the islands off Norway's western coast, which German merchant ships used to avoid running into the British navy. Finally, it was the Russo-Finnish "Winter War" which, in November 1939, afforded the Allies the opportunity of sending troops to Scandinavia for intervention on Finland's behalf.

OnFebruary 6, 1940 the German ship, *Altmark*, a supply vessel for the pocket battleship *Graf Spee*, was seen in Norwegian territorial waters. Believing she was carrying Allied prisoners, the British intercepted her, freeing 299 merchant seamen. This incident convinced Hitler that the Allies might act first in Scandinavia, and Lieutenant-General Nikolaus von Falkenhorst was immediately appointed to plan and lead the proposed conquest of Norway and Denmark. The operation was initially planned for March 20, but was delayed until April 9.

Meanwhile the Finnish surrender had brought the Allied plans for intervention on Finland's side to a halt,

and they decided to lay mines, landing troops only in response to German aggression while wholly underestimating the time that would be required to deploy in strength in the main Norwegian ports before the arrival of the Germans.

The German forces comprised two formations for the invasion of Denmark and Norway: the XXI Corps with two mountain divisions and five infantry divisions for the Norwegian part, and the XXXI Corps with the 170th and 198th Divisions for the Danish element. These two formations would be supported by all available warships and 41 troop transports, and in the air by the Luftwaffe with 290 bombers, 40 Stukas and 100 fighters. The element of surprise was necessary for success, yet most of the troops and their supplies had to be transported by sea. The German plan was thus based on the launch of a lightning attack on vital objectives, using fewer than 9,000 assault troops, and nowhere did an initial landing force exceed 2,000 men.

At about the same time, Allied troops destined for Scandinavia also embarked, and the British Home Fleet put to sea. The German preparations were in fact noticed, but the Norwegian government did not call for general mobilization. Thus, when the German invasion force slipped past the Home Fleet, it met no organized resistance on landing. As expected, Denmark succumbed within 24 hours on April 9; it was plain that the Danish government appreciated the military hopelessness of its position and it acceded to a German occupation in exchange for continued home rule. At most of the principal Norwegian ports, the assault troops landed without interference, or were delayed only slightly by brave but largely ineffectual resistance.

In Norway, the Germans landed at Kristiansand, Stavanger, Bergen, Trondheim, Narvik, and Oslo. In the process, two Norwegian coastal defense vessels were blown out of the water at Narvik; at Trondheim, the heavy cruiser *Admiral Hipper* and four destroyers forced the fjord entrance; at Bergen the cruiser *Königsberg* was damaged but landed enough troops to capture the town; Rear-Admiral Oskar Kummetz's force came under heavy fire in the long Oslofjord, and the *Blücher*, the German navy's most modern heavy cruiser, was sunk and the pocket battleship *Lützow* was damaged and compelled to withdraw. Consequently, half the force intended for Oslo was lost, but the city was taken by airborne troops. The sea route to Oslo was temporarily blocked, so that German supplies and reinforcements could not be landed, while Stavanger and its airfield at Sola were taken by paratroops.

At Narvik, the German 3rd Mountain Division disembarked successfully from ten destroyers, but neither its equipment or supplies arrived, nor did one of two tankers intended to refuel the destroyers for their homeward journey. The destroyers thus remained in the Vestfjord, leading to Narvik, where they were discovered at dawn on April 10 by Captain B.A.W. Warburton-Lee, commanding the British 2nd Destroyer Flotilla, who had taken the initiative by sweeping into the fjord. In the resulting battle, during which Warburton-Lee was killed, half the German destroyers were disabled or destroyed, the other half being destroyed three days later when another flotilla entered, led by the battleship *Warspite*. Some 2,600 German survivors joined the German forces on shore, and were supplied with weapons from a nearby Norwegian depot.

The assault phase left Denmark a conquered country, with German garrisons established in the major towns of Norway. The Allies had completely failed to prevent the landings, although they did achieve some success at sea. The battle-cruiser *Renown* damaged the German battle-cruiser *Gneisenau* on April 9; a British submarine sank the light cruiser *Karlsruhe*; and the *Königsberg*, damaged at Bergen, was later sunk by British naval aircraft.

The Germans at Narvik would have been unable to withstand an immediate Allied assault, and the Allied naval commander, Admiral of the Fleet Lord Cork and Orrery, favored such action. However, the land commander, Major-General P.J. Mackesy, disagreed, arguing that Narvik's harbor area was strongly fortified with light artillery and machine gun posts. Mackesy wished to take two unoccupied positions on the approaches to Narvik, where he could build up his forces until the snow melted and an

overland advance became feasible. The deadlock between the two British commanders, however, gave the Germans the time they needed to consolidate their position and score a moral advantage by claiming that the Allies had been brought to a standstill before Narvik.

The Norwegian commander in chief, General Otto Ruge, had the unenviable task of trying to hold the large areas of Norway still unoccupied by the Germans and regaining what the Germans had taken. Ruge believed he could hold out until Allied reinforcements arrived, and decided to retain as much as possible of the open country around Oslo where Allied troops, unaccustomed to mountain warfare and lacking the equipment for it, might be successful. But the Germans delivered reinforcements and equipment immediately Oslo was once again open to them, and Ruge's forces were threatened at too many points for him to concentrate more than a small proportion in any one sector. By mid-April, he could no longer hope to hold the Oslo area, and fell back to the northwest to make a stand to the south of Lillehammer in the Gudbransdalen and Osterdalen. Ruge believed that, in this region, his forces could hold the Germans long enough for the Allies to send major reinforcements, and also prevent the Germans in the south from linking up with those at Trondheim on the coast in the center of the country.

Only at this stage did the Allies begin to appreciate that the key to the reconquest of Norway was Trondheim, the port city which was the main link between the north and south of Norway. Therefore Trondheim joined Narvik on the list of major Allied objectives. The Allies planned a frontal assault on Trondheim from the sea, and a pair of subsidiary landings at Namsos, 80 miles (130km) to the north and at Åndalsnes, 150 miles (240km) to the south. Major-General A. Carton de Wiart commanded the Namsos force, comprising the 146th Infantry Brigade and a demi-brigade of French Chasseurs Alpins, while Brigadier H. de R. Morgan led the Åndalsnes landing with the 148th Infantry Brigade.

OPPOSITE: *The Germans were able to use only modest numbers of light tanks in the Norwegian campaign.*

RIGHT: *German troops land at a Norwegian port. The invasion of Norway required the use of nearly all of Germany's sea-lift capability, and the German navy suffered heavy losses in the process.*

Both landings were a success, but the British chiefs of staff then abandoned the frontal assault on Trondheim, which would have placed the fleet at risk. Instead, the northern and southern forces decided to close in on Trondheim from Namsos and Åndalsnes, where the forces already landed would be strengthened. But the Germans had already rendered the Allied thinking obsolete by their own program of reinforcement. The Luftwaffe had complete mastery of the air and the

The Scandinavian Conflicts

LEFT: The heavy cruiser, Admiral Hipper, and four destroyers, were responsible for the delivery of the army forces to take Trondheim.

BELOW: The Germans march British prisoners through Trondheim toward the port for shipment to Germany for incarceration as prisoners of war.

OPPOSITE ABOVE: The small northern Norwegian port of Narvik was central to Allied plans for the Norwegian campaign, but the small operation fought here revealed the Allies' lack of readiness for war against a skilled opponent such as Germany. Even so, the Germans lost 10 fleet destroyers in the two naval battles fought at Narvik.

OPPOSITE BELOW: In the Norwegian campaign, the Germans made the first use of airborne forces in combat operations, in this instance for the capture of Fornebu and Sola airfields outside Oslo and Stavanger, and later for the support of forces farther north.

The Start of World War II: The Flood of the German Tide

Allies were subjected to continual air attack, in which Namsos, in particular, afforded no protection. However, the Namsos force advanced to Verdal at the head of the fjord, some 50 miles (80km) from Trondheim, but there met a powerful German force on April 21, and withdrew in heavy snow. Carton de Wiart recommended that his force be evacuated, and this was accomplished on May 2–3 under heavy air attack.

In response to Ruge's request for reinforcement, Morgan and his 148th Infantry Brigade had advanced from Åndalsnes to Lillehammer to link up with the exhausted Norwegians. On April 24, Major-General B.T.C. Paget and the 15th Infantry Brigade reinforced them, with Paget assuming command. The Allies faced the Germans with determination, and there followed a series of bitter battles as the Allies were forced to fall back to Åndalsnes, from which they were evacuated on May 1.

All the Allied forces were withdrawn from the Trondheim area, as the Inter-Allied Supreme War Council had decided on April 26, to allow the Allied effort to concentrate on the recapture of Narvik. The Norwegians were greatly disappointed by the abandonment of central Norway, the superiority of the Germans now being perfectly obvious. The Allies had failed in the Trondheim area, and a mixed and improvised force of 6,000 Germans was by now holding 20,000 Allied troops at bay at Narvik.

Lieutenant-General Claude Auchinleck now arrived to take command of the Allied land forces in the Narvik area, whose withdrawal from central Norway meant that the Allied strength in this area could be increased, although some British troops were deployed to check any German attempt to advance overland from Trondheim.

Reinforcements included Major-General Marie Émile Béthouart's 1st Chasseur (Light) Division, two battalions of the French Foreign Legion, four Polish battalions, and 3,500 Norwegians. The German commander, Lieutenant-General Eduard Dietl, had also been reinforced and, on paper at

The Scandinavian Conflicts

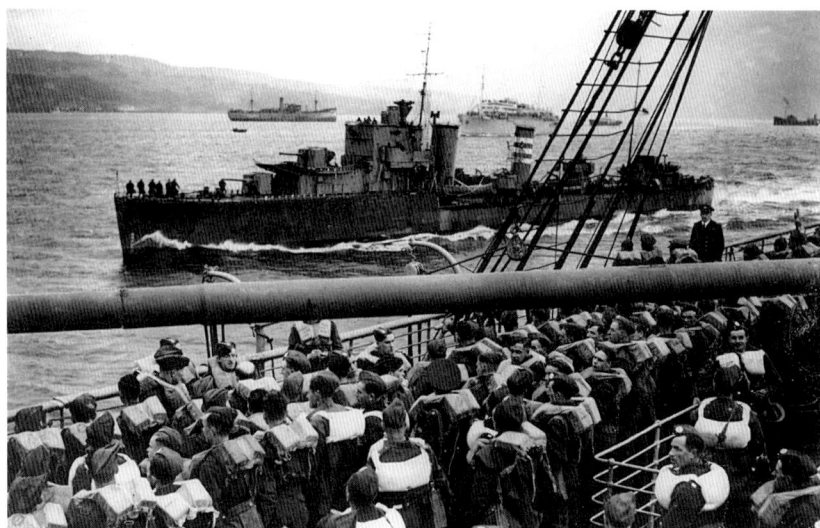

least, 13 Allied battalions faced 10 German battalions in the Narvik area. Dietl and Béthouart were both mountain warfare specialists.

At midnight on May 27 Béthouart led a force, with gunfire support from an all-British naval force, in an assault south across the Rombaksfjord, about a mile (1.6km) wide, while simultaneously, two Polish battalions attacked east on the south bank of the fjord. By 5:00pm,

LEFT: *Major-General Frederik Christian Essemann, commanding the Danish army's 2nd Jutland Division, emerges from his headquarters to surrender to the Germans on April 9, 1940.*

ABOVE: *British troops on their way back to the UK after one of the several evacuations of Allied troops from central and northern Norway in May and June 1940.*

LEFT: *German soldiers photographed in a captured Danish fort. Realizing the futility of trying to fight Germany's surprise invasion, the Danes capitulated without resistance in exchange for a measure of continued self-government.*

OPPOSITE: *German troops on the Arctic circle. Northern Norway was of strategic importance to Germany for its port of Narvik, whence Swedish iron ore was shipped to Germany, and as the launch point for the offensive into the northern USSR from June 1941.*

The Start of World War II: The Flood of the German Tide

the German garrison had retreated inland and Béthouart's forces were on the outskirts of Narvik. He then stood aside to let the Norwegian 6th Division enter the town. On June 7, the Germans found the Allies gone and the port installations demolished. The Allies had slipped quietly and secretly away in four convoys, between June 4 and 8, a move necessitated by the deteriorating situation in France.

The battle-cruisers *Scharnhorst* and *Gneisenau*, with the heavy cruiser *Admiral Hipper*, were in the area, however, and on June 8 a British tanker and armed trawler were sunk and the troopship *Orama* was hit. Later, the Germans spotted the British aircraft carrier *Glorious*, the fire of the *Scharnhorst* and *Gneisenau* setting her alight and also sinking the destroyer *Ardent*. Another destroyer, the *Acasta*, then launched a torpedo which severely damaged the *Scharnhorst*.

So ended the last action of the Norwegian campaign. On June 10 Ruge signed the surrender of the Norwegian army. The Germans had lost 5,636 men killed; the Norwegians had lost 1,335, the UK 1,869, and France and Poland about 530 between them. Although Allied action had not achieved its objective in cutting the iron route, or in reconquering Denmark and Norway, the action at sea meant that the losses suffered by the German navy would ultimately result in there being too few ships available for the proposed invasion of England.

Text-Dependent Questions

1. What was Hitler's justification in annexing the Sudetenland?

2. When did Hitler invade Poland?

3. When did the Soviet invasion of Finland begin?

Research Projects

What were the main causes of World War II?

WORLD WAR II

Chapter Three
GERMANY STRIKES TO THE WEST AND THE BATTLE OF BRITAIN

On May 10, 1940 the Germans forces began their largest operation to date in World War II. In one week, the Netherlands surrendered, Belgium had been largely overrun, and France was already talking of defeat. The offensive was not an operational surprise even if it did secure the element of a tactical one, the two sides being approximately equal in numbers of men and equipment. Until the beginning of 1940, the French commander in chief, General Maurice Gamelin, had been broadly correct in his conception of German strategy, and his defensive measures stood a chance of success. It was reckoned that the Germans would try for a lightning victory, based on the Schlieffen Plan of 1914, with the main attack coming through Belgium. Belgium had expressed its neutrality in 1936 but, unlike the Netherlands, had cooperated to some extent with the Allies in planning the defense of its eastern frontier. Gamelin prepared alternative plans for the Allies to advance the British Expeditionary Force (BEF) of nine divisions, under General Lord Gort, and the 1st French Army Group of 22 divisions, including two light mechanized ones, under General Gaston Billotte, to either the Dyle or Escaut rivers when the German invasion began. The French 9th Army, under General André Cora, would at the same time close on the right to the Meuse river, while the mechanized 7th Army, under General Henri Giraud, moved its seven divisions, including one light mechanized and two motorized, up the coast on the left flank to secure the Scheldt estuary and Antwerp. Gamelin hoped the Belgian army of 18 divisions would delay the Germans on the German/Belgian border in the region of Fort Eben-Emael, which was believed to be the strongest fortress in the world. The French believed the **Maginot Line** was strong enough a barrier on their own border with Germany, and were confident that no surprise attack could be launched through the forested hills of the Ardennes. Most of the remaining Allied field formations were deployed behind the Maginot Line in case of a breakthrough. The Allies were thus deployed with two strong flanks and a weak center, with their armor committed to the north.

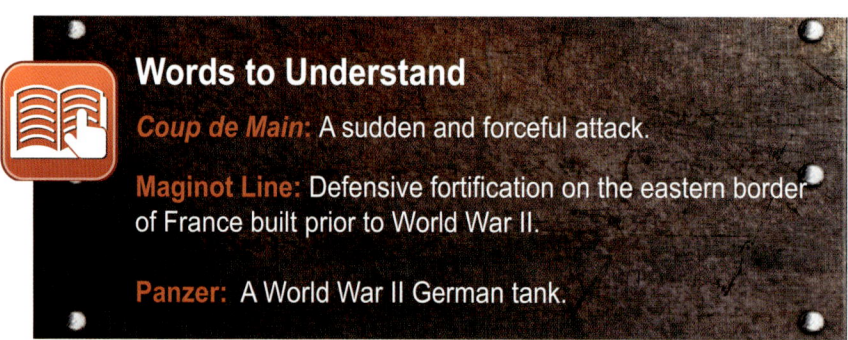

Words to Understand

Coup de Main: A sudden and forceful attack.

Maginot Line: Defensive fortification on the eastern border of France built prior to World War II.

Panzer: A World War II German tank.

LEFT: *The British prime minister in April 1940 was Neville Chamberlain, seen here at the time of the "Munich crisis" of September 1938, when Czechoslovakia was sacrificed for "peace in our time."*

OPPOSITE ABOVE: *French H-35 tanks on the move. The French had useful numbers of capable tanks, but these were deployed in "penny packets" to support the infantry, rather than concentrated and trained as decisive battlefield formations.*

OPPOSITE BELOW: *In the battle for France, the 7th Panzer Division was commanded by Erwin Rommel, seen here during a troop inspection.*

That the Germans planned to make their major attack though northern Belgium was true until the original plan was compromised and Lieutenant-General Erich von Manstein, the chief of staff of Army Group A, suggested that most of the Panzer divisions (and thus the main weight of the offensive) should drive through the center in the area of the Ardennes and thus through the weakest part of the French defense, while the Allied armies were drawn into north-eastern France and Belgium by the advance of Army Group B. After discussion at the Oberkommando des Heeres (OKH, or army high command), von Manstein's plan was approved by Hitler. For the offensive to the west, therefore, the German forces were deployed with Army Group A, commanded by Colonel-General Gerd von Rundstedt, and comprising 45.5 divisions (including seven Panzer and three motorized), with General Günther von Kluge's 4th Army from Army Group B sweeping through the Ardennes in the centre. The armor was organized as Panzergruppe "von Kleist," containing the XIX Panzer Corps under General Heinz Guderian; XLI Panzer Corps under General Georg-Hans Reinhardt; and XIV Motorized Corps under Lieutenant-General Gustav von Wietersheim; in addition, the 5th and 7th Panzer Divisions formed the XV Panzer Corps, under General Hermann Hoth, attached to the 4th Army. The armor was to act as a battering ram to thrust through the Allied lines in the Charleville-Sedan area and quickly push to the coast.

For the offensive against Belgium and the Netherlands, Army Group B was led by Colonel-General Fedor von Bock, consisting of 29.5 divisions, including three Panzer and two motorized. After von Manstein's plan was accepted, von Bock's forces were reduced in strength, making him naturally concerned that his two remaining armies would be equal to their tasks: the 6th Army was to force and cross the Albert Canal, and the 18th army to take the Netherlands, whose army totaled eight divisions. Army Group C, commanded by Colonel-General Wilhelm Ritter von Leeb, was

to attack with 19 divisions from southern Germany toward the Maginot Line, so pinning the French forces in the south.

The Germans thus totaled 134 divisions, including reserves, with which to face the Allies' 130 divisions. The French had as many tanks as the Germans, but the German armor was generally superior in qualitative terms, being better organized in specific **Panzer** divisions, and far superior in fast-moving armored warfare, having been designed and trained for independent operations with the Luftwaffe as support. The French were hampered in their belief, the result of their horrendous losses of World War I, that the fighting of a defensive campaign would result in fewer casualties, while the Germans were working to a brilliant plan, exploiting in full the capabilities of

their mobile forces to provide quick breakthroughs and thus the speedy defeat of their enemies for minimum manpower and matériel losses.

On May 9 Hitler ordered his forces to cross the frontiers of the Netherlands, Belgium, and Luxembourg at dawn on the following day. They achieved total surprise with their airborne attack in Belgium and the southern Netherlands, and for the first time airborne forces won a decisive victory more or less unaided, especially in their seizure of Fort Eben-Emael by a gliderborne *coup de main* attack. Allied troops were not brought to the alert until after the assault had begun, and by daylight on May 10, German paratroops had captured bridges around the Hague and Rotterdam in the Netherlands, together with the main airfields. The first of von Bock's three armored divisions advanced across the lower Maas (Meuse): the Dutch were unable to resist for long. The French 7th Army was trying to link with the Dutch army near Breda, but found the Germans already there and withdrew behind the Scheldt. The German 18th Army, under General Georg von Küchler, quickly overran the country and on May 15 the Dutch government capitulated after a devastating bombing attack on the city of Rotterdam.

Simultaneously with the attack on the Netherlands, the Germans pierced the Belgian frontier defenses, with General Walther von Reichenau's 6th Army attacking along the Meuse and the Albert Canal; airborne troops captured three of the main bridges along the canal immediately west of Maastricht. On the same day, in a brilliantly executed maneuver, German gliders landed on top of Fort Eben-Emael and the Belgian garrison surrendered. The Belgian army retreated to the line of the Dyle river as the Allies put their Dyle Plan into operation. The BEF advanced to the Louvain-Wavre position and the French 1st Army moved forward to Namur. One third of the French first-line armored vehicles were now on or behind this 22-mile (35-km) line linking Wavre with Namur. But to the south, in the 95 miles (155km) between Namur and Longeron, the French had only 12 infantry divisions; more importantly, only four cavalry divisions and two cavalry brigades were in position at the time of the German arrival. The French were short of antitank and antiaircraft guns, and ground defenses were lacking, especially around Sedan, the junction point of the French 2nd and 9th Armies. It was on these forces that the German Blitzkrieg (lightning war) offensive fell.

The British and French forces were still advancing into Belgium as Heinz Guderian and Major-General Erwin Rommel (leading the 7th Panzer Division) spearheaded the armored thrust through the Ardennes. Using the full width of the roads, the advance was rapid and no effective resistance was met

on the way through Luxembourg and the Belgian part of the Ardennes. On May 12 the Panzergruppe von Kleist and the XV Panzer Corps of Lieutenant-General Hermann Hoth reached the Meuse, from which the French cavalry, after a short delaying action, retreated after blowing up the bridges.

The XV Panzer Corps was on a more northerly route, heading for Dinant, and Rommel arrived here on May 12. The Panzergruppe von Kleist advanced toward Sedan, which fell to Guderian's XIX Panzer Corps as its defenders were hammered by Stuka and bomber attacks, while Monthermé fell to Lieutenant-General Georg-Hans Reinhardt's XLI Panzer Corps. The advance of Army Group A comprised the greatest concentration of tanks yet seen, which extended for more than 100 miles (160km) from end to end. The French were wholly bewildered by the pace and style of the German advance, which had been undertaken with great offensive spirit.

The Germans crossed the Meuse near Sedan and Monthermé, initially by infantry and motorcycle regiments, and pontoon bridges were then thrown across by the engineers for the vehicles of the Panzer regiments. The Germans had deliberately chosen to attack at the junction of the French 2nd and 9th Armies, where second-rate troops were deployed. On May 14, the 9th Army

OPPOSITE ABOVE: *German armor seen during a brief pause for rest, refueling and rearmament, during its high-speed punch through north-eastern France.*

OPPOSITE BELOW: *The Panzer forces comprised tanks for concentrated offensive effort, motorcycle teams for tactical reconnaissance, and trucks for the delivery of all-important fuel, ammunition, and other essential supplies including food for the men.*

RIGHT: *Built of concrete and tunneled deep into the ground, the Maginot Line was the heart of France's defense system. The Germans avoided it by the simple expedient of passing around its northern end though neutral Belgium.*

retreated 10 miles (16km), but the retreat rapidly became a panic-stricken flight. Guderian's bridgehead was now 31 miles (50km) wide and 15 miles (25km) deep. By May 16, the Germans were moving forward at the extraordinary rate of 40 miles (65km) per day. Guderian's XIX Panzer Corps then swept forward toward Abbeville and the southern coast of the English Channel, the tank commanders having been instructed to keep moving for as long as they had fuel. Thus, in four days, the Panzergruppe von Kleist and the XV Panzer Corps were able to destroy eight divisions from the French 2nd and 9th Armies and had opened a breach of some 80 miles (130km) in the French front.

The French had no real reserve with which to plug this gap, but the Allies, more importantly, had not fully grasped the implications of the situation in which they now found themselves, and thus stood no chance of sending what reinforcements they had to the places where they were needed most. The available reserves (22 divisions including three armored at the start of the campaign) were therefore deployed on a piecemeal basis, their movement toward the front being hampered by Luftwaffe attack. The Allies were often applying their minds to a situation which was at least several hours out of date, and relations between the powers were not ideal. The British and French forces,

between the North Sea and Luxembourg, were under Billotte's overall command; Billotte was not an effective coordinator, as a result of which communications were extremely difficult.

The Germans made very effective use of the Allied confusion to speed their advance, but then the Panzer divisions were ordered to halt. The German high command was surprised at the ease at which the Meuse had been crossed, and every day expected a French counterattack. Hitler wanted the Panzer divisions to wait until the arrival of sufficient infantry to provide flank cover along the Aisne river; von Kleist therefore ordered Guderian to halt on the night of May 15. Guderian protested, and after some argument the advance was resumed for a further day. On May 16, Rommel's 7th Panzer Division forced the Franco-Belgian border, quickly advancing to surprise Le Cateau at dawn the following day, thus achieving an advance of some 31 miles (50km), during which units of the French 18th Division and 1st Armored Division were scattered and the rear areas of the French 9th Army thrown into confusion. Next, Guderian was most surprised to receive a further order to halt. This time, von Kleist was decidedly hostile toward Guderian, who offered his resignation. General Wilhelm List, whose 12th Army included the Panzergruppe von Kleist, mediated and ordered Guderian to obey the halt command, but added that Guderian's formation could continue a "reconnaissance in force" to the west. Guderian construed this as allowing him to send the whole of his 1st and 2nd Panzer Divisions (two-thirds of his corps) which, on May 17, pushed a bridgehead across the Oise river at Muy. By May 19 the divisions had reached Péronne, and by nightfall on May 20 had reached Abbeville at the mouth of the Somme river. The motorized divisions were hard on Guderian's heels, assuming the defense of the sector along the Somme from Péronne to Abbeville, and providing flank protection against any attack from the south, as Guderian turned north. Guderian had already cut the BEF's lines of communication to its bases south of the Somme, and now desired to cut its line of retreat to the sea.

Von Rundstedt's Army Group A was now able to wheel north and northeast to trap the Belgian army, the BEF and the French 1st Army being in a pocket between his own army group and von Bock's Army Group B. However, von Rundstedt's southern flank, between the mouth of the Somme and Sedan, was very weak. This was noticed by the French, but they were too preoccupied with their attempts to restore their battered center to make any immediate response, especially as the very speed of the German advance gave them scant time to rally dispersed forces. Gamelin ordered a combined attack from north and south of the Somme to isolate the Panzer spearheads, but at this time Gamelin was replaced as commander in chief by General Maxime Weygand, who postponed the order while he assessed the situation. It was doubtful if the proposed

ABOVE LEFT: *German troops parade in triumph along the Champs Élysées in captured Paris. The city remained crushed beneath the German heel until August 1944.*

LEFT: *Adolf Hitler savors victory in Paris.*

OPPOSITE: *One of the mainstays of the German armored force in the first part of World War II was the PzKpfw III medium tank. This was reliable and well protected, but carried only modest offensive armament. The tanks pictured are those seen later in the middle part of the war, after side armor had been added to protect the upper part of the tracks, the running gear, and the junction of the hull and turret.*

attack would have succeeded, since the Luftwaffe had control of the air.

On May 19, the second of two local counterattacks by the incomplete French 4th Armored Division, under Colonel Charles de Gaulle, against the left flank of the XIX Panzer Corps between Crécy and Marle on the Serre river was successful in itself, but made little difference to the campaign as a whole.

Meanwhile the Allies were losing the campaign in Flanders. Weygand visited the northern group of armies, directing the BEF and part of the French 1st Army to counterattack towards Cambrai and Bapaume under cover of the Belgian army's retreat to the Yser river. Weygand's enthusiasm was giving the Allies the impression they were succeeding, and Gort had to explain that his troops, under great pressure from the east by Army Group B, could not break off and turn through 90° and move to the south. On May 21 Gort nevertheless had some success in a local assault on Arras. Two British light infantry battalions, a motorcycle battalion, and 74 tanks from the 4th and 7th Royal Tank Regiments, plus 70 French tanks, caught the 7th Panzer Division unawares, making Rommel believe he had been attacked by very strong forces with hundreds of tanks. But there was no attack from the south to complement the British effort from the north. Weygand ordered one on May 22, but communications were poor: the supreme headquarters did not even have a radio. The French 10th Army lacked the troops and ammunition to fulfil Weygand's orders, and the divisions were no longer where Weygand thought they were.

At Arras, however, the confidence of the Germans had been shaken and the high command was now convinced that the Panzer units were taking too many risks. Even so, Guderian's XIX Panzer Corps was in the process of striking north, isolating Boulogne on May 22 and Calais the next day, before pressing forward to the Aa river at Gravelines, only 10 miles (16km) from Dunkirk. Reinhardt's XLI Panzer Corps also reached the canal line from Aire to Gravelines via St. Omer, which was sparsely defended. There was then

nothing between the Panzer divisions and Dunkirk, the last port of escape for the BEF, but it was at this juncture that von Rundstedt ordered von Kleist to halt his armour: Hitler wanted to preserve it for the coming offensive south of the Somme, the land around Dunkirk being thought too marshy for tanks, and Field-Marshal Hermann Göring had affirmed that his Luftwaffe could achieve the task unaided. As was his propensity, Guderian protested, but this time the order was quite definite.

As the Germans delayed, the BEF escaped from Dunkirk. With such a desperate situation in Flanders, Gort had decided that the BEF must be evacuated, and the British government, headed by Winston Churchill rather than Neville Chamberlain since May 10, agreed. The withdrawal into the Dunkirk perimeter began, the French XVI Corps taking over its defense from the British. Vice-Admiral Bertram Ramsey planned the operation in which 338,000 men, including 113,000 French, were taken off the beaches at Dunkirk during the nine days up to June 4. Vessels of all types and sizes made the two-way journey across the Channel time and time again, braving Luftwaffe attacks off the coast of France. For the most part, however, the Royal Air Force was able to check the Luftwaffe and so prevent it from stopping or severely disrupting the evacuation. Allied troops were also evacuated from Boulogne, Le Havre, Cherbourg, St. Nazaire, and Bordeaux. In all, some 500,000 men were rescued during the month ending June 26. The Belgians had surrendered on May 28, having given the British time to withdraw to Dunkirk.

The Germans had suffered 60,000 casualties and captured more than 1 million prisoners in their lightning campaign. The Belgian and the Dutch armies had been destroyed, and the French had lost the support of 12 British divisions, most of whose equipment fell into German hands after the evacuation. Having lost 30 divisions, Weygand could now look to only 66 divisions, many of which were not at full strength, for the impossible task of defending the area from Abbeville to the Maginot Line. Two British divisions were still in France, south of the Somme, and two more would be sent over later.

The Germans had been given the time to bring up the mass of their marching infantry and reorganize. On June 5 they began their southerly assault with 140 divisions. The Germans' three objectives were to advance between the Oise and the sea to the lower Seine below Paris; to advance in a south-easterly

direction to defeat the French army in the Paris-Metz-Belfort triangle, and thus render useless the Maginot Line defenses; and to pierce the Maginot Line in the direction of Nancy-Luneville. Weygand deployed most of his remaining strength on the Somme-Aisne line, his troops posted in a series of strongpoints linked on the French maps but which, in fact, had large gaps between them where there was inadequate artillery cover. Both minefields and mobile reinforcements were sadly lacking. Weygand's plan to stand and fight was extremely inflexible and resulted in his troops often being by-passed or encircled by the Germans.

Army Group B attacked and crossed the Somme on June 5, while Army Group A attacked across the Aisne, where the French resisted with some determination but to no good effect. The Panzer divisions then fanned out in a southerly direction: the XIX Panzer Corps headed south and east toward the Swiss frontier; some elements of Panzergruppe von Kleist struck out to the south-east in the direction of Dijon, Lyon and the Mediterranean coast; and other units of the Panzergruppe von Kleist turned to the south-west toward Bordeaux.

The 4th Army attacked on the extreme right flank between Amiens and the sea, the 7th Panzer Division quickly reaching the Seine at Rouen. By now, the French armies were fracturing into unco-ordinated fragments. On June 14, Army Group C struck at the Maginot Line. The Luftwaffe supported the armored formations, bombing defended positions before the assault.

The imminent arrival of the Germans in Paris set off a new flood of refugees, causing congestion on the roads and providing targets for the Luftwaffe. On June 10, the French government left Paris for Tours, with Bordeaux as its ultimate destination. On June 14, German troops entered Paris, which had been declared an open city. On June 16, at a meeting of the French council of ministers, prime minister Paul Reynaud argued that resistance must continue, if necessary from abroad. He was supported by Brigadier-General de Gaulle (now the undersecretary of defense) but by few others, and therefore resigned. His successor was the aged Marshal Henri Pétain, a hero of World War I, who negotiated for an armistice.

The Panzer thrusts continued, and by June 22, the day of the French armistice, which came into effect three days later, the Germans had overrun all but southern France. The 7th Panzer Division had reached Cherbourg, while the 5th Panzer Division had driven on to Brest. The XVI Panzer Corps had taken Lyon and Grenoble, and the XIX Panzer Corps had reached the Swiss frontier and turned north-east to Belfort. The Maginot Line had finally crumbled.

With France's defeat now a certainty, the Italian dictator, Benito Mussolini, declared war on France, and on June 21 450,000 Italians attacked the French Alpine front. The 185,000 French troops deployed there successfully held off the Italians, and nowhere were they able to break through the French defenses, saving south-eastern France at least from Axis occupation. The Franco-German armistice was signed at Compiègne on the same site as the 1918 armistice, when Germany was the defeated power. Hitler allowed Mussolini to occupy Corsica, Savoy, and parts of Provence, while the Germans occupied northern, eastern, western, and south-western France, thus gaining control over the entire Atlantic and northern coasts of Europe.

It should be noted that in September 1940, Nazi Germany, Fascist Italy, and Imperial Japan signed the Tripartite Pact, which officially established the so-called Axis powers.

THE BATTLE OF BRITAIN

With the end of the fighting between French and German forces on June 25 1940, Germany's only still-active enemy was the UK. Convinced, up to this time, that Britain would either refrain from going to war or make only a token gesture, Hitler now felt that something would have to be done about the recalcitrant British, if they continued to deny the realities of the situation or refused his "last appeal to reason." Up to this time no serious planning for an invasion had been undertaken, and now the army and navy were at loggerheads over the way in which an invasion should be undertaken. The army wanted a major cross-Channel effort on a broad front, but the navy was unwilling to contemplate even a narrow-front assault across the Straits of Dover, so great had been its losses in the Norwegian campaign. Whatever type of assault was finally adopted, both the army and navy agreed that the essential prerequisite was command of the air to prevent the Royal Navy from cutting the invasion fleet to pieces, and to give the assaulting forces the necessary air support against the Royal Air Force.

Now promoted to the unique rank of Reichsmarschall, Hermann Göring was certain the Luftwaffe could fulfil this task, despite its losses in the French campaign. In fact, Göring's ambitions for his air force went further still: he was convinced that the Luftwaffe on its own

OPPOSITE ABOVE: The most pitiful victims of any war are the civilians, who are either caught up in the fighting or forced to flee ahead of it as refugees. These are French refugees photographed in May or June 1940.

OPPOSITE BELOW: The head of the Luftwaffe was Reichsmarschall Herman Göring (left), seen here in conversation with Werner Mölders, who was not only a superb tactician, but also a great fighter '"ace."

RIGHT: The standard German fighter throughout the first stages of World War II was the Messerschmitt Bf 109E, which was fast, agile, well protected, and moderately well armed.

could destroy the Royal Air Force and dominate the skies over southern England, thus persuading the British that continued resistance was futile and that they should seek a negotiated peace. But the Luftwaffe had been designed and steadily increased as a purely tactical air force, and Göring was now grandiosely entertaining its commitment in a strategic campaign, for which it was neither equipped nor trained, against the best air force the Germans had yet to meet.

So while the planning for the invasion continued, the Luftwaffe's three main formations were to start the battle to win air superiority if not outright supremacy: these were Luftflotte 5 under Colonel-General Hans-Jürgen Stumpff from bases in Norway; Luftflotte 2 under Field-Marshal Albert Kesselring from bases in the Low Countries and north-eastern France; and Luftflotte 3 under Field-Marshal Hugo Sperrie from bases in northern France to the west of the Seine river. Between them the three air fleets had some 3,600 aircraft, of which about 2,700 were serviceable on July 1.

Facing this formidable German strength was the RAF's Fighter Command, under the command of Air Chief-Marshal Sir Hugh Dowding: No.

10 Group, led by Air Vice-Marshal Sir Quintin Brand in the west of England; No. 11 Group, led by Air Vice-Marshal Keith Park in London and the south-east of England; No. 12 Group, led by Air Vice-Marshal Trafford Leigh-Mallory in East Anglia and the Midlands; and No. 13 Group led by Air Vice-Marshal Richard Saul in northern England and Scotland. At the beginning of July the squadrons of these four groups had an establishment strength of some 871 single-engined fighters, of which 644

were serviceable. Although the supply of aircraft from the factories and repair units would often cause concern during the forthcoming battle, the real problem was the acute shortage of pilots, despite the fact that other RAF commands, and even the Fleet Air Arm, had been combed for suitable replacements. But although it was considerably outnumbered, Fighter Command had certain distinct advantages: firstly there was radar and its associated fighter control system, backed up by visual observers stationed around the coast of Britain. This allowed fighters to be sent up in the right numbers and at the right time to intercept the most important German raids. Luftwaffe intelligence had underestimated the importance of this British control system, and the Germans thus failed to devote anything like sufficient attention to the elimination of the easily visible coastal radar stations.

Secondly, the British pilots were initially fresher than their opponents, and enjoyed the advantage of operating over their own country. Return flights to base with a damaged aircraft were relatively short, and pilots forced to bale out landed on friendly territory. The Germans, on the other hand, faced the gruelling flight back to the continent with damaged machines, or had to bale out over England or the Channel. From the latter they were usually fished out by the efficient British air-sea rescue service to become prisoners of war.

Thirdly, the key to domination of the skies over England lay with the fighters, and here again the RAF had an advantage: by the time the German fighters reached southern England, their length of time in the combat zone was tightly limited if they were to return to base without running out of fuel.

Fourthly, there was the question of the aircraft involved. The Luftwaffe's air strength for the Battle of Britain was divided into four main types: twin-engined bombers; single-engined dive-bombers; twin-engined heavy fighters; and single-engined fighters. The British relied mainly on Supermarine Spitfire and Hawker Hurricane single-engined fighters, which were slightly inferior to the Messerschmitt Bf 109 in terms of firepower but otherwise comparable in terms of agility and performance. This last was in the process of being improved by the large-scale introduction of constant-speed propellers. And once

ABOVE: *A British radar operator watches her display screen, ready to report any sign of German activity.*

LEFT: *The line of Chain Home radar stations, that eventually surrounded Britain's coast, provided adequate early warning of incoming Luftwaffe raids.*

OPPOSITE ABOVE: *The Germans placed great reliance on the Messerschmitt Bf 110 twin-engined heavy fighter and multi-role warplane. This had heavy armament and good range, but lacked the outright performance and agility to cope with the attacks of the RAF's Hawker Hurricane and Supermarine Spitfire single-engined fighters.*

OPPOSITE BELOW: *When operating in conditions of German air superiority, the Junkers Ju 87 Stuka dive-bomber proved very effective in destroying point targets. The Germans, however, did not have this advantage in the Battle of Britain and Stukas were savaged whenever they appeared.*

battle had been joined, the British fighters would prove markedly superior to the other three main classes of German aircraft.

There is no way of fixing a date for the definitive beginning of the Battle of Britain, but by July 1 it may fairly be said to have entered upon its first phase, with harassing attacks on British coastal shipping, ports and installations made by Luftflotten 2 and 3. The German plan was simple: by attacking these easily accessed targets with bombers, the British fighters were being drawn up into combat on terms favorable to the German fighters and decimated. Underestimating the real strength of Fighter Command, the Germans imagined the British would quickly begin to lose more aircraft than they could replace, and would thus be easy meat for the second phase of the German attack. The German plan backfired badly: the British fighters, positioned with the aid of radar, concentrated their attacks on the bombers and tried, wherever possible, to avoid combat with the German fighters, which in themselves posed no real threat to the UK as they carried no offensive armament. This coastal phase of the battle raged through July and the first week of August, and resulted in a serious setback for the Germans. Fighter Command's losses were acceptable, but German bomber losses were relatively heavy, and the Junkers Ju 87 dive-bomber, hitherto regarded as a war-winner, was revealed to be easy prey for single-engined fighters.

Hitler appealed to the UK to come to terms on July 29, but with the British refusal three days later the Germans began in earnest to prepare plans for the defeat of Britain.

On August 1 Hitler set the scene for the next phase of the battle by allowing attacks on the mainland of the UK from August 5 onward, the Luftwaffe taking the attack to the British forward fighter bases, coastal radar stations, and other targets in southern England. Poor weather delayed the start of the German offensive until August 8, and the second phase in fact lasted for only 16 days. Large numbers of relatively small forces wandered into southern England,

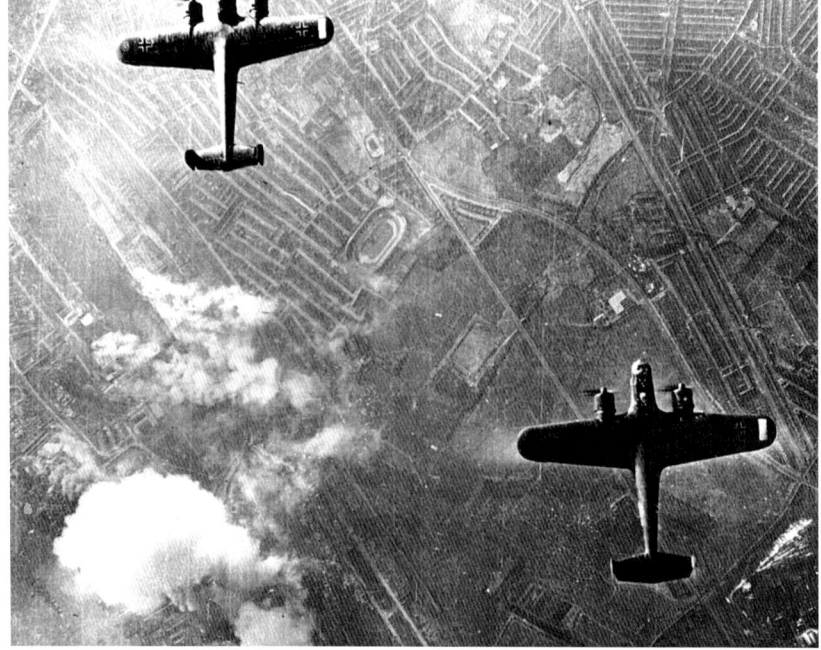

strafing airfields and ports to draw up the British fighter defenses and engage them in close combat. The brunt of the defense was borne by No. 11 Group which, because of the short warning time available, was only able to send up its squadrons individually or in pairs to meet the raids as they came in. Nevertheless, the British handled the German raids successfully, albeit at the price of quickly exhausting front line squadrons.

Dowding's genius was apparent at this time: he let his subordinates get on with their jobs, and concentrated with remarkable skill on keeping up the flow of pilots and machines to the squadrons which needed them; he also rotated new squadrons to the front at just the right moment to replace front line units on the verge of exhaustion. On the two main days of this second phase, August 8 and 15, the Germans made 1,485 and 1,786 sorties respectively, which Fighter Command was able to contain and also inflict severe losses on the Messerschmitt Bf 110 heavy fighters, as well as on the twin-engined bombers. At this time, British fighter tactics were in the process of transition from the prewar mass formations of 12 or more aircraft toward the German tactical concept of two pairs of fighters, each covering the other, while within each pair, one pilot took the lead with the other flying as his protective wingman. This was altogether more suitable in air combat between fast fighters, as it was tactically more flexible. The more numerous, but slightly slower Hurricanes, were in general tasked with the more important role of destroying the German bombers, while the Spitfires concentrated their efforts, to hold off the German fighters. The combination of target allocation, and the nature of the German tactics, was to prove a winner in the weeks ahead. Ending on August 23, the second phase of the battle left the British

ABOVE LEFT: *The nerve centers of RAF Fighter Command were its control rooms, such as this one at Stanmore Park, where data on incoming raids were received, processed, and used to dispatch the right squadrons to the correct locations for an interception.*

LEFT: *German Dornier Do 17 twin-engined medium bombers flying over London.*

OPPOSITE ABOVE: *Pilots rush to their Hawker Hurricane fighters as their squadron is scrambled to meet a German raid.*

OPPOSITE BELOW: *The Messerschmitt Bf 109E fighter of Franz von Werra, shot down over England where he was taken prisoner. In January 1941, von Werra was sent with other German prisoners to Canada, possibly becoming the only German airman to make his escape from there, returning to Germany via the still-neutral USA.*

in command of the skies over southern England and the Germans in some disarray as a result of their heavy losses.

The Luftwaffe now stepped up its efforts by introducing mass bomber formations into what became the third phase of the battle starting on August 24. The idea was for 100 or more bombers, in close formation and escorted by many fighters, to beat their way through to the British fighter bases and destroy them. The fighters would deal with any British aircraft that rose to intercept, and any RAF machines that escaped would find their bases destroyed. This third phase, which lasted to September 5, was the closest the Germans came to breaking Fighter Command, and the margin was very close indeed. Although the Germans again lost heavily, the British suffered the loss of over 450 aircraft and, more importantly, more than 230 pilots were killed or wounded. At the beginning of September, Fighter Command had very little left to throw into the fray: for the first time reserves were being used more rapidly than they could be replaced. It was at this stage that the Germans made their most significant error. Throughout this period, Bomber Command had been trying to carry the war to the Germans, attacking large concentrations for the projected invasion by day, and targets in Germany by night. For the first time, on August 24, Berlin was bombed. Hitler was so enraged that he ordered attacks on Fighter Command to cease, so that all

German efforts might be devoted to the destruction of London.

Just as the destruction of Fighter Command seemed imminent, therefore, the Luftwaffe switched to the daytime bombardment of London, this fourth phase of the battle beginning on September 7. Up to the end of the month, German bombers wrought considerable havoc on London, but Fighter Command was given some breathing time, with the result that both Nos. 11 and 12 Groups' squadrons could then concentrate on the massed German bombers and fighters. The destruction of these was great, and the supremely successful September 15 has since been celebrated as Battle of Britain Day. Losses at this rate were too heavy for the Luftwaffe to sustain, consequently on 1 October the last phase of the battle began. Fighter-bombers ranged over southern England by day, while bombers struck at London by night, but the tide against the Luftwaffe had now definitely turned. On 12 October, Hitler canceled his orders for the invasion of the UK and the Battle of Britain was won.

There was, of course, the Blitz on London and other industrial centers from November onwards, but the Battle of Britain was effectively over by 31 October. The British had lost 915 aircraft against the Germans' 1,733. In human terms, the Germans had fared even worse, for a large proportion of the losses had been multi-engine bombers. The UK had won the first strategic air battle in history, and had driven off the German threat of invasion.

The Battle of Britain

WORLD WAR II
Chapter Four
THE NAVAL WAR 1939–1940

While the period of inactivity along the Western Front between September 1939 and May 1940 was regarded by the newspapers as the "Phoney War," it was not so for the men of the U-boats, the Royal Navy and the merchant navy. From the morning of September 3, 1939, when the U-boats and surface ships, already at their war stations, received the signal from their high command, telling them that war with France and the UK had been declared, the shooting war began in earnest.

The British and French had planned cooperation, but it was the Royal Navy which took the lead in policy-making. Although Hitler had endorsed the international protocol banning unrestricted submarine warfare, or the sinking of merchant vessels without warning, and had given strict instructions to Commodore Karl Dönitz and his U-boat arm to obey the regulations, the Admiralty assumed the U-boats would not abide by the rules. This prediction seemed to be borne out when the liner, *Athenia*, returning to England on the first day of the war, was torpedoed by U-30 in the Western Approaches: this mistake arose from the belief, by the Germans, that it was in fact a troopship. As a result, the British initiated their full convoy system, and within a few weeks U-boats were sinking merchant ships on sight.

The U-boats had their greatest successes against warships, sinking the old aircraft carrier *Courageous* on September 17 and almost sinking the new aircraft carrier *Ark Royal*. On October 14 U-47 penetrated the waters of the Home Fleet's base at Scapa Flow in the Orkney Islands, sinking the old battleship *Royal Oak* in an undertaking whose propaganda value to the Germans considerably exceeded the naval importance of the destruction of an obsolete ship. But this episode had an important strategic effect, for it persuaded the British that the Home Fleet should abandon its main base until the defences of Scapa Flow had been further improved.

The heart of British naval strategy was the containment of the German navy in the North Sea by the laying of minefields in the English Channel and by the Home Fleet's control of the passage between the Orkney Islands and Norway. This policy of containment had worked admirably in World War I, and the Admiralty hoped to repeat its success while the resources of the British Empire were mustered to build up the country's strength. Conversely, if the German fleet should ever break out into the Atlantic, its ships would disrupt the convoys bringing raw materials and munitions from Canada and the USA, thus starving

the British Isles into submission. Luckily for the British, the German navy failed to exploit the temporary withdrawal of the Home Fleet in October–December 1939. Germany's two new battle-cruisers, *Scharnhorst* and *Gneisenau*, made a sortie from Wilhelmshaven on November 21, passed north of the Shetland and Faeroe Island groups without being sighted by British patrols, and attacked the armed merchant cruiser, *Rawalpindi*, which was patrolling off Iceland. In a hopelessly unequal fight the liner lasted for exactly 14 minutes and the German ships made their escape back to Germany. But the foray had done very little to break the British hold on the northern outlet to the North Sea and the Germans had been lucky to escape the concentration of forces which were in the vicinity.

The Germans had appreciated, even before the outbreak of war, how tight the British blockade would be, and to avoid this ensured that two pocket battleships, the *Admiral Graf Spee* and *Deutschland*, put to sea in the August before the outbreak of war. Once the Polish campaign was over, Hitler authorized attacks on British and French shipping, and soon the Admiralty was receiving reports of ships being sunk by unknown raiders all over the Atlantic. Eight hunting groups were formed, but only one of them had success, when on December 13 three cruisers caught the *Admiral Graf Spee* off the estuary of the River Plate on the eastern coast of South America. The German ship inflicted heavy damage on the largest British ship, the heavy cruiser *Exeter*, but the combination of three opponents was too much for the battleship, which sought refuge in the River Plate off the Uruguayan capital, Montevideo. Skillful British propaganda suggested that a capital ship and an aircraft carrier were

in the area, whereas only one more cruiser was available. The captain of the *Admiral Graf Spee* was ordered by Hitler to avoid the indignity of having his ship sunk, and Captain Hans Langsdorff scuttled the ship off Montevideo.

The Battle of the River Plate did much to hearten the British and little to encourage the Germans, the *Deutschland*

OPPOSITE: *The battle-cruiser* Scharnhorst, *together with her sister ship,* Gneisenau, *was one of the most important German warships of World War II.*

ABOVE: *A celebratory return to base for the U-47, after it had sunk the old British battleship,* Royal Oak, *at Scapa Flow on October 14, 1939.*

RIGHT: *Günther Prien, the commander of the U-boat U-47 when it sank the* Royal Oak.

The Naval War 1939–1940

having managed to get back to Germany after sinking only two ships. By the end of 1939 the British had checked the first German challenge to British control of the sea for the loss of only 15 merchant ships totaling 61,000 tons.

In home waters there was a new danger, however, in the form of the magnetic mine. The Germans, unaware that the British had their own, hoped to block British ports with a mine to which there was no known countermeasure. Losses were severe, including not only merchant shipping but also such important warships as the battleship *Nelson*, which was badly damaged while entering harbor. But the British soon discovered what was the appropriate solution to the problem: ships were quickly equipped with degaussing gear to neutralize the magnetism of their hulls. As the British already had a magnetic mine of their own, this first German attempt to gain a tactical advantage with what was supposedly a secret weapon was not successful.

The work of RAF Coastal Command's shore-based aircraft also played an important part in defending shipping from U-boat attacks, especially in the waters surrounding the British Isles. But the lack of suitable aircraft in adequate numbers, and more seriously the lack of a suitable weapon, robbed Coastal Command of a significant return for its efforts. The standard prewar bomb for the antisubmarine task was totally inadequate, and in the spring of 1940 a modified naval depth charge had to be introduced as an emergency measure. Fortunately for the British, this serious

technical limitation was matched by German problems with their torpedoes, which often failed to detonate on impact.

The German invasion of Norway in April 1940 put a definite end to the Phoney War. It took the British and French navies by surprise, although the first contact was made between an Allied force, on its way to lay mines in Norwegian waters, and the German invasion forces. Many opportunities were lost by the Royal Navy through bad planning and lack of coordination, and the devastating power of dive-bombers against warships came as an unpleasant shock. Nevertheless, it was the German navy which suffered more during the Norwegian campaign. At the outset, the new heavy cruiser, *Blücher*, was blown out of the water by Norwegian coastal defenses, while Fleet Air Arm Blackburn Skua dive-bombers sank the smaller cruiser, *Königsberg*, at Bergen. The two Battles of Narvik accounted for half the total German destroyer strength, a catastrophic loss which crippled subsequent German naval operations. The battle cruiser *Renown* surprised the new battle cruisers, *Scharnhorst* and *Gneisenau,* in a snow storm off the Vestfjord, scoring a damaging hit on one of them before they escaped. The two German ships later scored an easy kill when they encountered the British aircraft carrier, *Glorious*, as she was evacuating RAF personnel from northern Norway, while the *Scharnhorst* was crippled by a torpedo from one of the escorting destroyers. Neither did the *Gneisenau* escape without damage, for she was torpedoed by a submarine, thereby seriously depleting the strength of the German navy by June 1940.

The crisis in France in May and June 1940 meant an immediate end to the Anglo-French intervention in Norway, and soon the ships were involved in the enormous problem of evacuating troops from France, in an undertaking that rescued 338,000 British and French troops, but at a heavy cost in ships sunk or damaged. For a time it seemed as though Hitler might really invade the British Isles, and the Royal Navy's entire resources were devoted to what many saw as a last-ditch stand. Only afterwards was

The Start of World War II: The Flood of the German Tide

OPPOSITE ABOVE: The Admiral Graf Spee, *burning after the ship had settled on the shallow bottom of the River Plate estuary.*

OPPOSITE BELOW: Captain Hans Langsdorff, convinced that the British had brought in additional ships, including an aircraft carrier, scuttled the Admiral Graf Spee *in the River Plate estuary before killing himself.*

ABOVE: The commander in chief of the German navy until January 1943, when he was succeeded by Admiral Karl Dönitz, was Grand Admiral Erich Raeder.

RIGHT: A British warship bombards the port of Cherbourg in northern France. Once it had been taken by the Germans in June 1940, the port made a useful base for German coastal forces operating in the English Channel.

it clear that the German navy had suffered far too heavy casualties in Norway to be capable of supporting a seaborne invasion, and when the Luftwaffe failed in its attempt to destroy the RAF, the threat of invasion gradually receded. It would have eased the minds of the British defenders to have known that the strongest opponents of the proposed invasion were Hitler's naval staff.

The situation after Dunkirk was nonetheless extremely gloomy for the British. Not only were they now faced with the Italians in the Mediterranean, without the help of the French navy, a vital element of prewar strategy, but they also faced a hostile coast, whose ports now accommodated German surface and subsurface forces, stretching from Bordeaux to the Arctic Circle. The Royal Navy's strategic position of September 1939 had been outflanked to the north, west, and south, and if the Germans had possessed a stronger navy, with more understanding of the principles of sea power, they could have forced the recalcitrant British to negotiate an armistice. The gravest consequence for the British was that the U-boats were now able to operate from the Bay of Biscay, a fact which left them more fuel once they had reached the convoy routes. As a result, a huge strain was brought to bear on the already hard-pressed escort forces.

The end of the Norwegian campaign and the defeat of France marked the beginning of what would be known as the Battle of the Atlantic, which was to rage essentially unabated for five years. It was not only the most vital maritime campaign of the entire war but also possibly the most importantly strategic of all, the Atlantic being the means by which the U.S. and the UK were linked. Had the Atlantic lifeline been cut, the industrial might of the U.S. could not have been brought to bear against Germany, and the essential supplies provided by Canada and the USA would have been un available to the British.

Fortunately, the British had taken timely steps before the war to remedy their weakness against U-boat attack The existence of the Asdic sonic underwater detection equipment was suspected by the Germans, but nothing was actually known about it until after the fall of France. A massive program of cheap utility convoy escorts, the corvettes had been started in 1939, and the first of these was ready in April 1940. In conjunction with the timely realization of how radar could be used, these countermeasures proved to be just in time to stave off disaster.

WORLD WAR II

Chapter Five
THE WAR IN AFRICA

THE ITALIANS ARE CHECKED IN NORTH AFRICA

At the time of Italy's entry into the war in June 1940, there were some 236,000 Italian troops under the overall command of Marshal Rodolfo Graziani in North Africa. The Italian 5th Army was in western Libya, and in the east was the Italian 10th Army, under General Mario Berti, consisting of the XXI and XXII Corps with three infantry divisions, one Blackshirt division, and one native Libyan division. The Italians had 1,811 guns, 339 light tanks and 151 first-line aircraft. The British commander in chief in the Middle East, General Sir Archibald Wavell, had five divisions (some 100,000 men), but of these only 36,000 men were in Egypt as

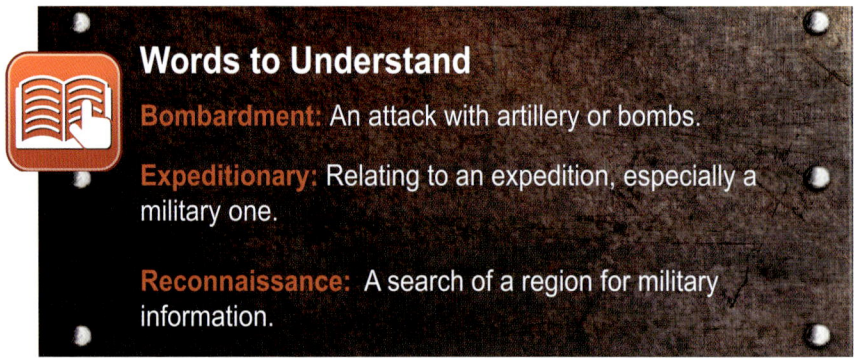

Words to Understand

Bombardment: An attack with artillery or bombs.

Expeditionary: Relating to an expedition, especially a military one.

Reconnaissance: A search of a region for military information.

the strength of two incomplete divisions: Major-General M. O'Moore Creagh's 7th Armored Division with two brigades, and Major-General P. Neame's (from August Major General N. M. de la P. Beresford-Peirse's) Indian 4th Division with two infantry brigades and part of its artillery. The British had 225 armored vehicles. On June 8 Lieutenant-General Richard O'Connor assumed command of all troops in the Western Desert Force, later to be renamed the XIII Corps.

The desert produced nothing for the support of armies. There were no roads, except along the coast, although there were a few recognizable tracks. Skilled driving could overcome the difficulties of desert terrain, but good navigation was essential in a practically featureless landscape. The British forces felt more at home than the Italians, and possessed some measure of vital desert sense. The British kept the Italians off-balance with frequent raids into Cyrenaica by elements of the 7th Armored Division. Graziani was under pressure from Mussolini, the Italian dictator, to take the offensive, but felt that his army was not ready. Thus it was only on September 13 that the 10th Army finally went over to the offensive. Two Italian columns advanced, one along the coast through Sollum, the other through the desert south of the escarpment parallel to the coastal strip, although it soon gave up this exposed route, moving through the Halfaya pass onto the coastal strip. The small British covering force fought an unhurried battle for four days as it withdrew, firing on

The Start of World War II: The Flood of the German Tide

OPPOSITE: *General Sir Archibald Wavell was the British commander in chief in the Middle East between August 1939 and July 1941.*

RIGHT: *The British armor was technically superior to the Italian armor it faced, but was modest in numbers, poorly supplied with spares, and operated by units which often failed to understand the real nature of armored warfare in the context of the Western Desert.*

BELOW: *The Italian tank force in North Africa had a number of moderately useful medium tanks, but placed far too great a numerical and operational significance on its CV-33 light tanks, which were cheap to produce but of no real operational value.*

the Italian columns which presented excellent targets. On September 16 the Italians reached and occupied Sidi Barrani, where they halted, Graziani's main concern at this stage being the construction of a metaled road and a pipeline back to the border in order to receive supplies and water.

The British expected the Italians to push straight on to Mersa Matruh, and planned to attack them when they moved. Meanwhile, the Italian positions at Sidi Barrani were bombarded by the Royal Navy and bombed by the Royal Air Force. In October the British situation in the desert was improved by the arrival of the Matilda I infantry tanks of the 7th Royal Tank Regiment. Designed specifically for the support of infantry, the Matilda I had armor proof against Italian antitank guns. The 2nd Royal Tank Regiment and the 3rd Hussars also arrived at this time. Wavell was now planning a short, swift raid against Sidi Barrani, and from this idea there developed an ambitious plan for a far-reaching offensive. On October 28 the Italians moved against Greece, and Wavell now had to do without certain of his resources, which were transferred to help the situation there. He was therefore

Benito Mussolini
Benito Mussolini, Italy's leader, was a vainglorious Fascist who was deposed in 1943. He was later restored to power over the rump of a Fascist state in northern Italy, and was killed ingloriously by partisans in 1945.

45

anxious for immediate action against Sidi Barrani. Wavell's daring plan called for the penetration of a 15-mile (25-km) gap in the defenses of Sidi Barrani in the area where the rocky terrain had prevented the Italians from building an antitank ditch, leaving an gap which they could not properly cover for their lack of adequate numbers of mines and antitank guns.

This Operation Compass entailed detailed logistical and tactical planning, in that it would be necessary for some units to cross 75 miles (120km) of open desert. The Matilda I tanks would have to penetrate the Italian defenses at night to avoid detection, and moonlight would be necessary if the forces were to get into formation after the move through the desert. Dumps of ammunition and supplies were placed halfway between Nibeiwa and Mersa Matruh, and all preparations were made under conditions of the greatest secrecy. The training of the troops was accomplished by way of exercises, which provided valuable experience. Only a few people knew that exercise number two on December 9 was to be the real attack.

While a force under Brigadier A.R. Selby attacked along the Maktila coast road, the British 7th Armoured Division and the Indian 4th Division struck through the gap in the Italian defenses at dawn on December 9. One battalion attacked near Nibeiwa at 5:00am to draw the attention of the Italians to this non-essential sector, while the Indian 11th Brigade, 7th Royal Tank Regiment, with 48 tanks, and the divisional artillery of the Indian 4th Division with 72 guns, slipped through to form up beyond for the attack. Surprise was complete: at 7:00am the artillery shelled the camp at Nibeiwa and the tanks approached the north-west entrance, destroying 20 unmanned Italian tanks before bursting into the camp with the infantry in their wake. The Italians fought sporadically, their artillery being the most resilient, but gave up when they were unable to stop the advance of the tanks. By 10:40am it was all over: 2,000 Italians had been taken prisoner and 35 tanks were in British hands.

The 7th RTR then wheeled north with the Indian 5th Brigade to attack the fortified camp known as Tummar West, which was held by the 2nd Libyan Division. This fell at 4:00pm. On the following day, the Indian 4th Division cleared Tummar East following a spirited Italian resistance.

During the evening of December 9 the 7th Armoured Division reached the sea, isolating the survivors of Tummar, and cutting the road from Sidi Barrani west to Buqbuq. The Italian pocket at Maktila had also been cleared. Sidi Barrani itself fell during the evening of December 10 after it was subjected to naval bombardment. On December 11 the Indian 4th Division crushed the remaining resistance east of Sidi Barrani and the 7th Armoured Brigade cut off the 64th Catanzaro Division, caught on the move between Buqbuq and Sollum. The British, for 624 casualties, had taken 38,300 prisoners, 237 guns, and 73 tanks.

Much to O'Connor's dismay, the Indian 4th Division was then transferred to Sudan and was replaced on December 18 by Major-General I.G. Mackay's Australian 6th Division. But without waiting for the arrival of the Australians, O'Connor launched his remaining force in pursuit of the disorganized Italians. On December 16 the Italians evacuated Sollum and all posts on the Libyan-Egyptian frontier, falling back to Bardia. The 7th Armoured Division and the British 16th Brigade followed up, cutting the road linking Bardia with Tobruk farther to the west. The Italian XXIII Corps, commanded by Lieutenant-General Annibale Bergonzoli, was ordered to hold Bardia with 45,000 troops. The defenses of Bardia, on an 18-mile

LEFT: *A Universal (or Bren-gun) Carrier leads a British heavy artillery tractor past a Fascist monument on one of the few roads in North Africa. The desert campaign was largely dependent on the availability of fuel for the various forces' motorized and mechanized equipment.*

OPPOSITE ABOVE: *An Italian antiaircraft gun in North Africa. The British were able to secure and maintain air superiority over the Western Desert until the Germans arrived in February 1941, when there developed a see-saw numerical and technical battle before the British regained almost complete air superiority later in 1942.*

OPPOSITE BELOW: *The Italian air force made extensive use of aircraft such as the SIAI-Marchetti SM.82 to deliver urgently needed supplies across the Mediterranean as the British aircraft, submarines, and surface warships based on Malta began to decimate the Italians' ability to convoy ships across to North Africa.*

(30-km) perimeter, were new and complete, with strongpoints located at about every 820yds (750m), an anti-tank ditch 13ft (4m) wide and 4ft (1.25m) deep, and dense barbed wire entanglements and minefields.

O'Connor had only 23 tanks left for lack of adequate spare parts. For the attack on Bardia, therefore, he decided that the infantry must cross the antitank ditch over a special assault bridge, clearing the mines with the aid of engineers to allow the Matilda I tanks to exploit the breach. At dawn on January 3 the attack was launched, with 120 guns and naval and air bombardments in support. The Australian 6th Division entered the ditch and the tanks rolled across the bridge into Bardia, meeting only ineffectual resistance. The efforts of the Italian air force were destroyed, and on January 4 the Allies reached the sea, having cut the Italian garrison in two. The Italian forces surrendered to the XIII Corps, yielding 45,000 prisoners, 460 guns, 131 tanks and 700 trucks.

The next objective was Tobruk, with its deep-water port and the nearby El Adem airfield, which were to be captured intact. The defenses of Tobruk had not yet been completed and extended along a perimeter of about 40 miles (65km). The Italian defense was based on the XXII Corps, consisting mainly of the 61st Sirte Division with 25,000 men. Tobruk had already been surrounded after an unopposed advance by the 7th Armoured

Division. The Australian 6th Division joined it and the attack began at dawn on January 21. The Australians broke into the perimeter south of Tobruk and the Matilda I tanks then entered the breach and took the Italians by surprise. The defense made a few counterattacks with some spirit, but the battle was over by nightfall. There was little damage to the harbour, and the seawater distillation plant remained intact. Some 25,000 Italians and their weapons were captured.

The 7th Armoured Division then advanced towards Mechili and on January 24 the 4th Armoured Brigade engaged the Italian tanks, knocking out nine while the others escaped. On the same day, the Australian 6th Division made an appearance at Derna.

The Allies had done remarkably well to advance so far. The logistic problem of maintaining the advance had been enormous, but O'Connor had wanted to keep the Italians off-balance. On January 29 the Italians evacuated Derna. O'Connor ordered the Australian 6th Division to continue its pressure in the coastal region while the 7th Armoured Division advanced towards Msus. But the Allies had only 50 cruiser tanks left, most of which needed a major overhaul. O'Connor wished to await the arrival of two regiments of the British 2nd Armoured Division, scheduled to reach him at any time, but air **reconnaissance** revealed signs of the Italian evacuation from Cyrenaica, which, if this was to be intercepted, required immediate action. Graziani by now had lost heart, having suffered the disappointment of seeing his tanks beaten at Mechili.

The retreating Italians used the coast road, while the Allies, cutting

The War in Africa

across from Mechili to Beda Fomm, had to cross rough desert. Creagh's advance was headed by a mechanized all-arms column, whose 50- mile (80-km) trek was making a slow advance. The armored cars of Lieutenant-Colonel J.F.B. Combe's 11th Hussars reached Msus on 4 February. On the next day, they and the 2nd Battalion, The Rifle Brigade, arrived south of Beda Fomm, positioning themselves astride the road down which the first Italian column would come marching from Benghazi. Confused fighting raged throughout the following day, with burning tanks littering the site. The Allies were helped by the fact that the Italian tanks had arrived in small groups, making them easy targets. The British tanks had maneuvered into good firing positions, using the lie of the land to their advantage, while the Italians were unable to coordinate an effective counterattack, and another 20,000 Italians were captured.

The British finally reached El Agheila. The XIII Corps, with two under-strength divisions, had overcome the huge logistical problems of advancing 560 miles (900km) and had destroyed the nine divisions of the Italian 10th Army.

THE GERMANS ENTER THE NORTH AFRICAN FRAY

Lieutenant-General Erwin Rommel arrived in Tripoli on February 12, 1941 with the leading elements of the small German force Hitler had reluctantly agreed to supply in an effort to save the Italian North African "empire." At this time Lieutenant-General Richard O'Connor was planning an immediate advance from El Agheila to Sirte and thence to Tripoli, but General Sir Archibald Wavell was instructed that Cyrenaica must be secured with the smallest possible force so that more units could be sent to support the Greeks. Wavell envisaged no danger from the

Germans before the summer, and deployed the 2nd Armoured Division, Indian 3rd Motorized Brigade and Australian 9th Division in Cyrenaica. Rommel found the Italians preparing for a stand at Sirte with one incomplete armored division and four infantry divisions, mostly without artillery. As his

ABOVE: Italian infantry surrender.

OPPOSITE ABOVE LEFT: Erwin Rommel (left). dominated the way in which the Axis forces fought this campaign.

OPPOSITE ABOVE RIGHT: Field-Marshal Jan Smuts visiting South African Troops in North Africa.

OPPOSITE BELOW: German artillery in action during the Axis forces' unsuccessful siege of Torbruk from April 1941.

Deutsches Afrika Korps arrived, Rommel moved elements of its 5th Light Division forward to a position some 20 miles (32km) west of El Agheila. It was his wish to attack early in May, but he was ordered to wait until the 15th Panzer Division arrived.

By the end of March, 15 Axis convoys had delivered 25,000 men, 8,500 vehicles and 26,000 tons of supplies in Tripoli, despite harassment from the Royal Navy and the Royal Air Force, and Rommel persuaded the Italians that Tripolitania, to the west of Cyrenaica in Libya, could be held with German help. At dawn on March 24, the reconnaissance group of the 5th Light Division and the Italian Ariete Division attacked El Agheila. The British defenders pulled back without a fight, taking up new positions at Mersa Brega, which Rommel attacked on March 31 with the aid of some 50 Junkers Ju 87 Stuka dive-bombers. Rommel encountered some resistance but the British retreated, their columns streaming back in some disorder toward Benghazi and Mechili. Many armored vehicles broke down and the British could not prevent a substantial body of German and Italian troops advancing north along the east coast of the Gulf of Sidra and fanning out to the northeast in the general direction of Tmimi. For days, Rommel exploited his success

without informing his superiors and, in less than a fortnight, forced the British to give up most of Cyrenaica with the exception of Tobruk. In the process, the Germans also took a number of important prisoners, including O'Connor, who had been found hopelessly off course on his way by car to Tmimi.

Wavell decided that Tobruk must be held: Major-General L.J. Morshead and the Australian 9th Division, plus other elements, withstood several attacks by Rommel's forces. On the night of April 13–14 the Germans cleared a way through the antitank ditch and the 5th Light Division's armor moved forward from the south with infantry riding on the tanks and moving up behind them. The infantry was annihilated by the Australian artillery and 250 German prisoners were taken. Rommel was furious and on April 16–17 personally directed the Ariete Division in another attempt, which was again unsuccessful. A further attack by the 5th Light Division between April 30 and May 4, in the area of Bir el Madauar and Giaida, farther to the west, was also a failure.

Meanwhile, the 15th Panzer Division had taken Bardia on April 12, which was unoccupied along with Forts Capuzzo and Sollum, but then found its way to Egypt blocked by forces under the command of Brigadier W.H.E. Gott. With his forces thus dispersed, Rommel was instructed to await reinforcements before again attacking Tobruk. At the same time, the British were delivering about 100 tons of supplies into Tobruk every day. The arrival of the 15th Panzer Division concerned Wavell, but British reinforcement arrived via the "Tiger" convoy of fast merchant ships: on May 12 43 Hawker Hurricane fighters and 238 tanks, made up of 135 Matilda I, 82 cruiser and 21 Mark VI light, were unloaded at Alexandria, all of this being vital to Operation Battleaxe, which Wavell was planning for the relief of Tobruk. Wavell's forces now comprised the Western Desert Force under Lieutenant-General Sir Noel Beresford-Peirse, including the Indian 4th Division, 7th Armoured Division and the 22nd Guards Brigade.

In the second half of May, Operation Brevity was launched in the area of Halfaya, Sollum, Capuzzo, and Bardia, and although not a success in itself, Brevity provided useful experience. The Battleaxe plan was for an advance on a 20-mile (32-km) front between Sollum and Sidi Omar, with infantry and a brigade of infantry tanks on the right, and a brigade of cruiser tanks and support groups on the left. Wavell hoped to secure this area, defeat the Axis troops laying siege to Tobruk and, finally, perhaps to advance to the area of Derna and Mechili. The forces besieging Tobruk were mostly Italians, the 15th Panzer Division guarding the Libyan-Egyptian frontier and the 5th Light Division deployed on the coast between Tobruk and the frontier. The number of men, guns, and tanks on each side was roughly equal. The Germans were well supplied with antitank weapons, however, including about 12 3.465-inch (88-mm) dual-purpose antiaircraft and antitank guns, which could stop any British tank at a distance of 1,640 yards (1500m), well beyond the effective range of the tanks' own guns.

Operation Battleaxe began on June 15 with the Royal Air Force bombing of the German forces. The British advanced but Rommel committed only a small part of his armor, while making excellent use of his guns to inflict major losses along the flanks of the British effort. The 7th Armoured Brigade took Capuzzo, then things began to go wrong for the British. The Indian 11th Brigade and the 22nd Guards Brigade failed to take Halfaya, and in the evening the 7th Armoured Brigade clashed with the 5th Light Division, in the process being trimmed to a strength of just 37 fit tanks. The next day saw rapid movement and hard fighting, during which Rommel launched two counterattacks. Heavy fighting occurred around Halfaya, and the 7th

The Start of World War II: The Flood of the German Tide

Armoured Brigade fought a running battle with the 5th Light Division down to Sidi Omar. Rommel then struck east, hoping to surround the Western Desert Force and thus preventing the British from uniting their forces, and crippling a good many tanks in the process. On June 17 the British called off the offensive, having by this time a mere 22 cruiser and 17 infantry tanks available to them.

OPPOSITE: *British infantrymen double past a knocked-out German tank during the see-saw fighting of the North African campaign.*

ABOVE: *German troops, including a paratrooper (in a coat and with a shallow-brimmed helmet), take a look at an Italian antiaircraft gun position.*

Wavell withdrew the British and commonwealth forces before their last line of communications was cut by Rommel, having lost 1,000 men, plus 22 cruiser and 64 infantry tanks. Wavell was now replaced by General Sir Claude Auchinleck, who arrived on July 1.

The date for Auchinleck's first effort, Operation Crusader, was November 18, the objective being yet again the relief of Tobruk. Auchinleck organized his strength as the 8th Army, under the command of Lieutenant-General Sir Alan Cunningham. The British believed the key to the successful relief of Tobruk lay in the destruction of the two Panzer divisions, but Cunningham was uncertain of how best to seek and win a decisive armoured battle. By mid-November, the 8th Army of six divisions and six independent brigade groups contained the greatest concentration of armor yet achieved by the British, with 724 tanks at the front and 200 more in reserve. On the right flank was the XIII Corps (ex-Western Desert Force) under the command of Lieutenant-General A.R. Godwin-Austen, with the New Zealand Division, Indian 4th Division and 1st Army Tank Brigade. On the left flank was the XXX Corps under the command of Lieutenant-General C.W.M. Norrie, with the 7th Armoured Division with 473 tanks, the 4th Armoured Brigade Group, the South African 1st Division and the 22nd Guards Brigade Group.

Possessing an armored strength of about 400 tanks, the Axis force comprised the Italian XX (Mobile) Corps with two divisions; the DAK with

reconnaissance in force and kept his armor back at Gambut, which denied Cunningham the armored battle in which he expected to achieve a significant victory. The 7th Armoured Division then moved forward to Sidi Rezegh, just outside the Tobruk perimeter, and here was counterattacked by the 21st Panzer Division. Meanwhile, the 4th Armoured Brigade Group remained at Gabr Saleh to guard the XIII Corps' right flank. Plans went ahead for the breakout, on November 21, from Tobruk, where Major-General R.M. Scobie now commanded a British and Polish garrison centered on the 70th Division. Rommel, accordingly, rushed his armor to the Sidi Rezegh area to prevent the breakout.

So began a most confusing battle. For three days tanks, armored cars, and infantry and artillery attempting to drive south from Tobruk, were opposed by the German and Italian forces watching the perimeter, which were in turn counterattacked by the British 7th Armoured Brigade supporting the breakout. The German armor attacked in its turn, having rushed from Gabr Saleh. The battlefield extended for 20 miles (32km) and was often obscured by clouds of dust. Each side used tanks captured from the other.

Rommel became impatient with the slow pace of the battle, and on November 24 set off at the head of the 21st Panzer Division, with 100 tanks from the area of Bardia to reach the Mediterranean by way of Sidi Omar and a wheel 180° to the left, so striking the British in the rear. But he had no significant success and overextended his lines, the 21st Panzer Division having been strung out along the Trigh el Abd with its forward units at Sidi Suleiman.

the 15th Panzer Division, 21st Panzer Division (ex-5th Light Division), Afrika Division and Italian Savona Division, together with the Italian XXI Corps with four divisions. The Afrika Division and four Italian divisions were surrounding Tobruk, with the 15th Panzer Division behind and to the east of them. One Italian division was deployed in the frontier area with the 21st Panzer Division astride and to the south of the Trigh Capuzzo.

Cunningham planned to employ the XIII Corps, consisting mostly of infantry and a tank brigade, to pin the Axis forces in the forward area, while the more mobile XXX Corps crossed the undefended frontier south of Sidi Omar, from where it would advance toward Tobruk or Bardia. The "Crusader" attack began at dawn on November 18 in torrential rain, and the XXX Corps advanced to Gabr Saleh. However, Rommel thought that this was only a

LEFT: A German soldier poses for the camera with North African children.

OPPOSITE: Though fast and agile, the Crusader cruiser tank generally suffered from the same limitations as most British tanks of the period, namely armament that was inferior to that of opposing tanks.

The action deteriorated into a series of sporadic bouts wherever Rommel appeared to take personal command. On November 26 the German tanks withdrew into Bardia. Meanwhile, the British reorganized, and both collected and repaired significant numbers of knocked-out tanks. On November 26, Auchinleck replaced Cunningham as commander of the 8th Army with Lieutenant-General N.M. Ritchie, but directed the battle personally; the British forces south of Tobruk made good progress, forcing Rommel to return his tanks back into the fray.

The Axis forces were now on the verge of exhaustion, and Rommel retreated after some confused engagements south of Tobruk; no more supplies could be delivered to him before the end of December. On December 5 Rommel withdrew his forces east of Tobruk and a general retreat began the next day, with Rommel's rearguards fighting methodical delaying actions, which XIII Corps could not simply brush aside. The British reached Benghazi on December 25, the Germans fighting vigorously at Agedabia before withdrawing to El Agheila. The XXX Corps reduced the Axis garrisons near the Egyptian frontier, and 15,000 prisoners were taken at Bardia on January 17, 1942. For the loss of 17,700 men and sizeable numbers of armored vehicles, the British and commonwealth forces had relieved Tobruk, gained invaluable combat experience, driven the Axis forces from Cyrenaica, and inflicted some 38,000 casualties on them.

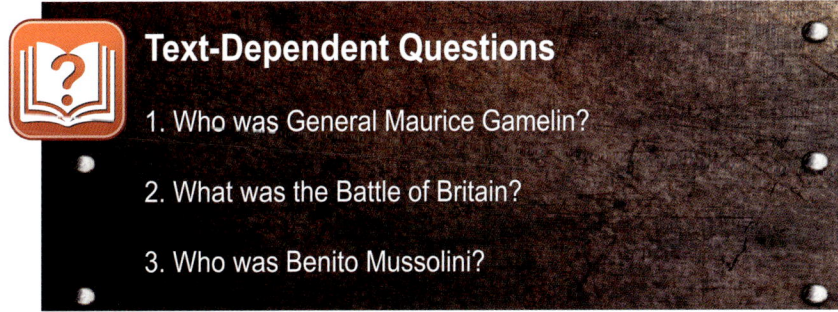

Text-Dependent Questions

1. Who was General Maurice Gamelin?

2. What was the Battle of Britain?

3. Who was Benito Mussolini?

Research Projects

What was Field Marshal Erwin Rommel's role in World War II?

WORLD WAR II

Chapter Six
GERMANY TAKES YUGOSLAVIA AND GREECE

The Balkan campaign was planned by Hitler as a direct result of Italy's failure to gain success against Greece, which Benito Mussolini's forces had invaded in October 1940. German troops had already entered Bulgaria, which signed the Tripartite Pact on March 1 1941, the Greek government rightly inferring that Germany was planning an invasion, leading them to request help from the UK. On February 14, 1941 General Sir John Dill, the Chief of the Imperial General Staff, and Anthony Eden, the Foreign Secretary, flew to Cairo to assess the situation with local commanders, and a conference was held in Athens on February 22 with Greek political and military leaders. It became clear that the UK was lacking the strength both to help Greece and to ensure victory in Africa at this time. Yet the British government knew full well that an offensive against the Axis forces was needed to prevent them from crushing Greece, so giving Hitler a stronger case in his attempts to persuade Turkey to join the Axis powers. There were two elements in the British commitment to the defense of Greece: first, the dispatch of an **expeditionary** force consisting of 58,000 British, Australian, and New Zealand troops, together with 100 tanks, to the Greek mainland; and second, the establishment of a combined British and Greek defensive force consisting of some seven divisions under the command of Lieutenant-General Sir Henry Maitland Wilson, along the Aliakmon Line stretching from the mouth of the Aliakmon river, north of Mount Olympus, to the Greek-Yugoslav frontier near Flórina. Greek troops were also to be deployed to hold a weaker Metaxas Line north of Serrai in Macedonia to delay any German offensive from southern Bulgaria toward Thessaloníki. A further 13 divisions

The Start of World War II: The Flood of the German Tide

would continue to hold the Greek-Italian front in Albania between the Ionian Sea north of Sarande and Lake Okhrida via Tepelenë.

These positions left the extreme southern part of the Yugoslav-Greek border, the so-called Monastir gap, exposed to any German advance from the southern part of Yugoslavia, at the time a neutral zone, a fact that caused dispute at the conference. There were insufficient divisions to plug this gap effectively, and the conference decided to communicate with the British ambassador in Yugoslavia for an assessment of the situation and a request to the Yugoslav government for the protection of the frontier and the prevention of any German movement from south-western Bulgaria. The only contingency plan available, should the Yugoslavs fail, was to hold the Olympus mountains and withdraw south-west towards Grevena to block the Monastir-Flórina valley route.

Events in fact moved with a speed that overtook the Allied planning for a defense of the Monastir gap. German pressure on Yugoslavia to become an ally proved sufficient, and Yugoslavia signed the Tripartite Pact on March 25. Then an anti-Axis coup by a small band of Yugoslav officers, led by a former chief of the air staff, General Dusan Simovic, offered the Allies some hope. This was short-lived, for an angry Hitler was now determined to destroy Yugoslavia. So superior were the German forces that Hitler declared war on Yugoslavia and Greece simultaneously on April 6, 1941, a mere week behind his original schedule, the defeat of Yugoslavia taking just 12 days. German troops swept through the country and then into the north-eastern part of Greece before Wilson's forces had completed their defenses along the Aliakmon Line.

The German forces in Yugoslavia comprised the 2nd Army in the north, and the 12th Army, together with General Ewald von Kleist's 1st Panzergruppe in the south-east. The Germans were supported in the extreme north-west by the Italian 2nd Army and in the center by the 3rd Army of Hungary, which had signed the Tripartite Pact on December 12, 1940 as its fourth member. Possessing only obsolete weapons, the Yugoslavs were in indefensible positions themselves. On April 6 Belgrade was heavily bombed and a Blitzkrieg offensive began. The right-hand elements of the 1st Panzergruppe covered 310 miles (500km) in seven days down the valley of the Morava river to Belgrade. By April 8 its left-hand formation, the XL Panzer Corps, had taken Skopje, the next day reaching Prilep, and armored units entered Thessaloniki on April 10. From the north the 14th Panzer Division rushed through Zagreb, driving south toward Sarajevo, which it seized on April 15. The morale of the Yugoslavs was very low, and the government surrendered the country on April 17. However, many Serbs refused

OPPOSITE: *Field-Marshal Wilhelm List commanded the German 12th Army, which from starting points in western Bulgaria advanced into south-eastern/central Yugoslavia and Greece from April 9, 1941.*

ABOVE: *German officers take in the sights of conquered Athens from the Acropolis.*

RIGHT: *German paratroops on Crete, while suffering very high casualty rates, nevertheless succeeded in taking the island.*

55

to admit defeat and continued to fight the Germans under the command of Colonel Draza-Dragoljub Mihailovic.

The Greek resistance was more stubborn. The Army of Macedonia took on the German XXX Corps and XVIII Mountain Corps, which entered northern Greece from southern Bulgaria on April 6. There was severe fighting in the region of Kelkayia and Istibey.

German forces also approached through Yugoslavia: the 2nd Panzer Division crossed the Greek frontier at dawn on April 8 and advanced to reach Thessaloníki on the same day. The SS Leibstandarte Adolf Hitler Brigade swept into the Monastir gap, the collapse of the Yugoslavs bringing the right wing of the German 12th Army, under Field-Marshal Wilhelm List, up to the

Aliakmon Line. Wilson was compelled to withdraw the expeditionary force from the coast near Mount Olympus through Kozam up to the Siatista pass and on to Lake Prespa. The left flank of this arc was weak and included several large gaps. This new position could not be held, and as the Germans pushed through the Aliakmon valley Wilson, on April 16, ordered his forces to fall back to Thermopylai, on the instructions of the Allied commander-in-chief, Field-Marshal Alexandros Papagos. The German XVIII Mountain Corps crossed the Aliakmon Line, bypassed Mount Olympus, and reached Larissa on April 18. At the same time the XL Corps forced a breach between the left of the British forces and the right of the Greek armies retreating from the Albanian front. The SS Leibstandarte Adolf Hitler Brigade captured Grevena on April 21, continuing forward to effect the capture of Ioánnina.

The situation was clearly beyond Allied redemption, and on April 19 British and Greek generals agreed that, in the best interests of both countries, the British and commonwealth expeditionary force should be evacuated from the Greek mainland. Rear-Admiral H.T. Baillie-Grohman made the arrangements for the withdrawal, and despite the fact that the Luftwaffe had control of the air and all embarkations had to be made at night, the operation was successful. Four-fifths of the British troops, more than 50,000 men, including some Greeks and Yugoslavs, were evacuated. Again, as at Dunkirk, all the heavy equipment had to be abandoned. The majority of the evacuees were taken straight to

ABOVE LEFT: *Major-General Bernard Freyberg (right), a New Zealander, was the Allied commander on Crete.*

LEFT: *The workhorse of the German air transport arm was the Junkers Ju 52/3m, but this suffered very heavy losses during the German airborne invasion of Crete.*

OPPOSITE: *German troops cross a river in Greece using a commandeered local boat.*

Alexandria in northern Egypt, but some went to Crete to swell the Allied garrison on that island. On April 24 16 Greek divisions surrendered to the Germans at Thessaloniki.

Crete was strategically significant in the Mediterranean in that Suda Bay, on its north coast, was an ideal fueling base for the Royal Navy between Malta and Alexandria, and also in the fact that the airfields at Máleme, Rétimo, and Heráklion also provided a supply link with Tobruk, the focus of British resistance in the Middle East. Hitler also realized the strategic value of the island, and on April 25 ordered the planning and execution of Operation Merkur, in which Crete was to be taken by a colossal airborne assault led by Lieutenant-General Kurt Student, the man who initially developed this type of tactic. He commanded the newly created XI Fliegerkorps, which included the 7th Parachute Division with three infantry regiments. The air support needed for the operation was provided by the VIII Fliegerkorps, commanded by General Wolfram von Richthofen. The forces available for Merkur included 500 bombers and fighters, a similar number of transport aircraft, and 72 DFS 230 assault gliders. The primary objectives were the three airfields.

The defense of Crete was based on one British infantry brigade supported by numbers of Greek, Australian, and New Zealand units evacuated from Greece. By the time the assault began, the Allied force numbered some 42,000 men, although was poorly coordinated as a result of the island's indifferent communications, lacked cohesion, and was woefully ill-equipped. The Greek evacuees had brought some light weapons with them, but there were very few heavier supporting weapons: for example, there were only 68 antiaircraft guns to protect an island 160 miles (260km) long, while tools and signaling equipment were also scarce. Air support for the ground forces was minimal: the RAF in the Middle East had suffered heavy losses in past months, and by 19 May, after heavy **bombardment** from the Germans, there were only seven operational aircraft left on the island. This inadequate defense force was entrusted to Major-General B.C. Freyberg on April 30, giving him little time to prepare.

After the defenses of the three airfields had been subjected to air attacks, the Germans began their

operation on May 20. Paratroops of the 7th Fliegerdivision were dropped on the approaches to the airfields at Rétimo and Heráklion, and to the west of the town of Caneá. It was intended that the landings should take place where there were few defenders, but inadequate German intelligence meant that the paratroopers arrived in areas where there were Allied defenders. There was intense fighting, especially in the area of Máleme, where the Germans landed among the New Zealand 22nd Battalion. None of the three airfields was taken on the first day as planned, and the Germans were unable to back the invasion with sufficient supplies. Their problem was exacerbated by the failure of two German convoys to land troops and stores on the island on May 21 and 22, the result of the interception of the convoys by three Allied cruisers and their accompanying destroyers, which sank ten ships before the rest of the German convoys fled in disorder without landing any men or equipment. The Royal Navy paid heavily for its successes: two cruisers, the *Fiji* and *Gloucester*, and two destroyers, the *Juno* and *Greyhound*, were sunk by air attack, and other ships were badly damaged by wave after wave of German bombers.

By May 24 the air attacks were making it impossible for the Royal Navy to continue its patrols near Crete in daylight. Admiral Sir Andrew Cunningham, commanding the Mediterranean Fleet, could no longer guarantee the prevention of German seaborne landings. But Student was still

ABOVE LEFT: *Men and vehicles of the German 12th Army on the move in Greece.*

LEFT: *The Greek navy's two battleships in April 1941 were the* Kilkis *and* Limnos, *ex-U.S. Navy pre-Dreadnought ships of no real operational value. Both ships were sunk by German dive-bombers.*

OPPOSITE: *Greek officers at the surrender of Greece. The Greeks fought with determination but were short of many essentials when faced by skilled opponents fielding the latest weapons.*

faced with the problem of taking the airfield at Máleme. His orders were that the Gruppe "West," commanded by Major-General Eugen Meindl, was to be concentrated to take Máleme, and that the 5th Mountain Division was to land and join the troops at Prison Valley in the Chania region: together they were to take Caneá and Suda on the western and eastern sides of the isthmus linking the Akrotiri peninsula to the rest of Crete. On May 21, therefore, Student concentrated his forces at the perimeter of Máleme airfield, while Lieutenant-General Julius Ringel's mountain troops landed under heavy fire on the airfield itself. These troops managed to break out of Máleme and establish contact with the German forces in Caneá, taking the town on May 27.

This final push by the attackers persuaded Freyberg that Crete could not be held, and he asked for permission to order an evacuation. This involved the movement of about 20,000 men, in the form of 4,000 from Heráklion on the north coast and the rest from Sfakia beach on the southern coast. On May 28 the troops were lifted from Heráklion. It took until June 2 to complete the evacuation, by which time the cruiser *Calcutta* and the destroyers *Hereward*, *Kashmir*, *Kelly* and *Imperial* had been sunk. Some 800 troops and the ships carrying them failed to reach safety.

The fight for Crete had been bloody: the Allies lost 1,800 soldiers killed, a similar number wounded, and 12,000 taken prisoner. Royal Navy casualties amounted to 1,828 men killed and 183 wounded as well as three cruisers and six destroyers. One aircraft carrier, three battleships, six cruisers, and seven destroyers were also damaged to a greater or lesser degree. Yet for the Germans this was a Pyrrhic victory, for they had lost almost 7,000 men out of an invasion force of 22,000, with 200 aircraft destroyed. Invasion by air, on this scale, was still very much a novelty, and the results were awaited in Germany with keen interest. In the event, the scale of the losses, especially among the elite troops of the airborne arm, were so great that Hitler steadfastly refused to authorize any similar operation after this time. Thus plans for an airborne invasion of Malta were abandoned by Hitler in June 1942.

The Greek campaign had been largely a political gesture, undertaken by the British and commonwealth forces largely for political reasons, namely the desire of the British government to show that it was willing to support an ally, and so help Turkey in its refusal of German blandishments. In overall terms, however, it had been a very costly 56 days, and the commitment to Greece had effectively prevented the British and commonwealth forces in North Africa from achieving a major strategic success.

WORLD WAR II

Chapter Seven
OPERATION BARBAROSSA: THE GERMAN INVASION OF THE USSR

On November 5, 1937 Hitler revealed to his senior military commander and Joachim Ribbentrop, the foreign minister, that his long-term ambitions in Europe were the seizure of the Lebensraum needed for a greater German state, by force if necessary, for the requirements of the German people were paramount. In light of this decision, which involved all people of German ethnicity as well as German nationals, Hitler announced that between 1938 and 1943 both Austria and Czechoslovakia were to be taken, Poland was to be defeated and occupied and, finally, the USSR was to be invaded and conquered. Those present to hear Hitler's monumental plan were totally thunderstruck for, among other things, the German armed forces were completely unready for even the smallest part of this huge scheme, even allowing for the expansion that was continuing. The professional military men were also distressed by the fact that Hitler had wholly failed to take into account the

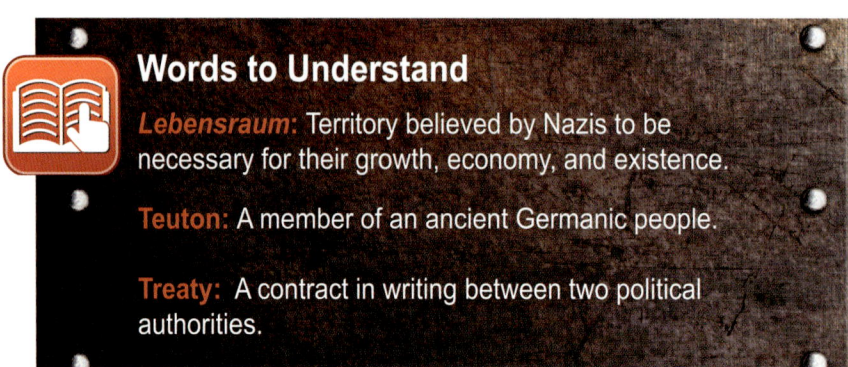

Words to Understand

Lebensraum: Territory believed by Nazis to be necessary for their growth, economy, and existence.

Teuton: A member of an ancient Germanic people.

Treaty: A contract in writing between two political authorities.

probable intervention of France and the UK once the nature of Hitler's concept had become clear.

But despite their fears, Hitler's plans met with initial success, despite the intervention of France and the UK. By the end of 1940, of Hitler's targets only the USSR was left, the UK remaining steadfast in its refusal to accede to a German victory. It should be noted, however, that while the concept of *Lebensraum* was the avowed reason for the German expansion, and Germany's victories in 1939–40 were rich in resources, another less overtly stated factor in the German leader's thinking was his long-established hatred of Communism. In Hitler's mind, therefore, the defeat of the USSR would at one and the same time serve to spearhead what he believed to be the western world's inevitable crusade against the "disease" of Communism, to lead to the destruction of the racially inferior Slavs by the superior Teutons, and to secure all of the USSR's territory and resources for the

LEFT: Movement of heavy equipment by draft animals was still very much the norm in the first years of the war on the Eastern Front, and the pace of operations was determined largely by that of marching men and plodding animals.

OPPOSITE ABOVE: A PzKpfw III medium tank and supporting infantry in a blazing Soviet town.

OPPOSITE BELOW: Expecting the 1941 campaign to be over before the onset of the Russian winter, the Germans were poorly equipped for winter campaigning and were forced to make use of every item of Soviet winter clothing they could seize.

The Start of World War II: The Flood of the German Tide

Josef Stalin
The USSR was ruled with an iron hand by Iosef Stalin, a man in many ways as evil as Adolf Hitler, but whose ruthlessness and determination in the second half of 1941 helped to save the USSR from defeat by Germany.

benefit of the German people. Thus was Germany committed to the largest military undertaking of modern history, a huge and complex series of campaigns which would decide the outcome of World War II. For it was in the huge areas of the USSR's western reaches that Germany was to deploy the majority of its forces against a Soviet war machine that, after devastating military reserves in the second half of 1941 and first half of 1942, grew enormously in size and capability to the end of World War II in 1945.

Germany's approach to the war with the USSR reveals Hitler's political astuteness at its most effective. In 1939 he wished to have no distractions as he dealt with the rest of Europe, so a Russo-German Non-aggression Treaty was signed in Moscow on August 23, confirming in its secret terms that the USSR was to invade Poland shortly after the Germans had launched their own campaign from the west, and take the eastern portion of the country. At the same time, Germany was to provide USSR with technical assistance in return for raw materials and foodstuffs. With the possible threat to his east thus obviated, Hitler could then turn his undivided attention to the problems of France and the UK. Thus Germany was able to launch its attack to the west in April and May 1940 in the knowledge that there was no threat to its eastern borders. But throughout this time Hitler was nonetheless thinking of the great enemy that he must crush. His preoccupation with planning the defeat of the USSR was not evident during the Battle of Britain, though after the war it emerged that even if the Luftwaffe had succeeded in gaining air supremacy over the southern part of the UK, Hitler would probably not have ordered an invasion as he needed to husband his forces for the

Operation Barbarossa: The German Invasion of the USSR

Adolf Hitler Speech "Europe together against Bolshevism"

onslaught, even though this was finally delayed and weakened by the late decisions to secure Germany's southern flank by taking Yugoslavia and Greece. Yet even before the formal postponement (in fact abandonment) of the invasion of the UK, German land forces were being moved from north-west Europe across Germany and German-occupied Poland toward the new German-Soviet frontier created by the conquest of Poland. Although apparently only a minor issue at the time, the abandonment of the plan to invade the UK was, with the decision to attack the USSR, one of the two most important, and ultimately fatal, grand strategic decisions taken by Hitler, for it condemned Germany to a two-front war, something he had said he would never entertain.

Planning for Operation Barbarossa began in December 1940. Despite their shock at the audacity and sheer size of the task confronting them, German military planners worked with their accustomed professionalism to produce a variety of plans. These were examined and successively discarded, their best features worked into the definitive plan that slowly emerged. The date set for the start of the invasion was May 5, 1941, which would give the German armies a good campaigning season through the summer and fall before the onset of the terrible Russian winter. The plans developed all through the spring of 1941, the troops trained, and all that was necessary for the campaign was massed with the greatest secrecy along the frontier with the USSR. All was ready for the start except for one thing: the German armies knew what they had to achieve at the tactical and operational levels, but the high command was operating in something of a strategic void as it could not get Hitler to commit himself to a stop line. The German armies were thus condemned to surge forward eastward into European Russia, while the high command could only hope that the Soviets would capitulate after its major cities had been overrun. Hitler refused to entertain any consideration of the USSR's implacable determination to survive, and had fixed no final objective for his men. The nearest the Germans came to establishing a strategic goal was the occasional mention of a vague line running from Arkhangyel'sk, on the White Sea in the north, to Astrakhan at the mouth of the Volga river on the Caspian Sea in the south. The Germans thus embarked on Barbarossa with the clear political goal of destroying the USSR and seizing its land and resources, but with a totally unclear military objective, which was to bedevil the efforts of the troops in the field.

Barbarossa was huge and bold. Three German army groups were to invade the USSR. In the south, Field-Marshal Gerd von Rundstedt's Army Group South comprised the German 6th, 11th and 17th Armies, the Romanian 3rd and 4th Armies, General Ewald von Kleist's 1st Panzergruppe (five Panzer and three infantry divisions), and two Hungarian divisions, and was to crush all the Soviet forces between the Black Sea and the Pripyet marshes. In the center, Field-Marshal Fedor von Bock's Army Group Center comprised the German 4th and 9th Armies together with General Heinz Guderian's 2nd Panzergruppe (five Panzer and four infantry divisions) and General Hermann Hoth's 3rd Panzergruppe (four Panzer and three infantry divisions), and was to advance on the Warsaw-Smolensk axis and then press on to take Moscow. In the north, Field-Marshal Wilhelm Ritter von Leeb's Army Group North comprised the German 16th and 18th Armies as well as General Erich Höpner's 4th Panzergruppe (three Panzer and three infantry divisions), and was to drive through the Baltic states to take Leningrad, the spiritual home of Bolshevism. Farther north again, Finland, a co-belligerent rather than ally, was to commit its forces, under the command of Marshal von Mannerheim, to retake the Karelian isthmus and threaten Leningrad from the north, as well as driving toward Lake Onega to cut the Soviet rail communications with Murmansk in the far north. Here Colonel-General Nikolaus von Falkenhorst's Norway Army was to drive toward Murmansk. In all, the German plan envisaged the advance of some 3 million men, of whom 250,000 had been provided by satellite countries, in 162 divisions along a 2,000-mile (3200-km) front. As usual, the major tactical scheme to be used was the now-standard pincer movement, in which the armor broke through and then closed behind the enemy's main forces, trapping them and then pressing forward, while the trapped forces were mopped up by the slower-moving infantry which, like the bulk of the artillery and logistic forces, still relied heavily on horses. Four months were considered sufficient for this huge undertaking.

The Soviets were heavily deployed along the same frontier, for despite the non-aggression treaty, Iosef Stalin had few illusions about Hitler's long-term plans. In the south was Marshal Semyon Budenny's South-West Front of six armies (52 infantry and 20 tank divisions) facing Army Group South. In the centre was Marshal Semyon Timoshenko's West Front of three armies (30 infantry and 8 tank divisions) facing Army Group Center, and in the north was Colonel-General F.I. Kuznetsov's

OPPOSITE: *German troops start to cross the German-Soviet border on June 22, 1941 on a corduroy road typical of those used in the western part of European Russia at this time.*

ABOVE: *Men of the 2nd SS Infantry Division Das Reich move through a burning Soviet village during the summer of 1941. Later a Panzergrenadier and finally a Panzer division, "Das Reich" was one of 38 Waffen-SS divisions to see service in World War II, gaining a reputation for superb fighting qualities but also notoriety for its savagery and war crimes.*

RIGHT: *A Soviet officer briefs his men.*

(soon Marshal Klimenti Voroshilov's) North-West Front of two armies (20 infantry and 4 tank divisions) facing Army Group North. In the far north, facing the Finns and the Germans, were three Soviet armies. The Soviets also had some 3 million men, with another million in garrisons throughout the rest of the USSR. Once the war had started, mobilization began to increase this number rapidly. The main trouble with the Soviet forces, however, was quality rather than quantity, for Stalin's purges of the mid and later 1930s had robbed the armed forces of most of their best commanders. The Soviet soldier was adequately trained in the basics and very durable, but lacked initiative and had

Operation Barbarossa: The German Invasion of the USSR

weapons inferior to those of the Germans. The two most notable exceptions to this last were the artillery and the new T-34 medium tank. The inferiority of Soviet weapons was most notable in the Soviet air forces, whose sole world-beater at this time was the Ilyushin Il-2 ground-attack warplane, available as yet in only small numbers, and the prototypes of a number of other advanced warplanes. The Soviet forces were massed along the frontier rather than deployed in depth, which greatly helped the German pincer tactics, the standard Soviet tactics calling for attacks after large numbers of troops had been massed, which made it all but impossible for the Soviet troops to counter the German armored pincer movements.

With preparations on the German side almost complete, there occurred an episode typical of Hitler and which completely jeopardized Barbarossa. This was Hitler's decision that Yugoslavia and Greece would have to be subjugated before the invasion of the USSR was committed, with the result that Barbarossa forces were bled of the resources to defeat these two nations. This also meant that Barbarossa itself had to be postponed by five weeks, a delay that cut into the already short campaigning season, with disastrous results, the start of Barbarossa now being scheduled for June 22, 1941.

Prefaced by the standard artillery and air bombardments of the Soviet front-line ground and air forces, the German armies headed east at 3.00am. At the tactical level surprise was total, and nowhere did the Germans encounter anything but the most limited opposition as they broke through what was in effect a cordon defense. Soviet warplanes were caught on the ground and destroyed in huge numbers by the Luftwaffe's fighters and bombers, while the modest numbers which managed to get into the air were easily destroyed by German pilots with far greater operational experience, flying qualitatively better aircraft. On the ground, most of the Soviet forces were caught completely unawares by the speed and power of the German advance and were quickly overrun or bypassed. The Soviet forces, cut off in groups of up to an army in size, were contained by the German infantry and then destroyed. Hopeless though their prospects were, most of these Soviet pockets fought with great courage and determination, their resistance serving a purpose in slowing the German advance.

One of the major problems faced by the Germans was the complete disparity in the speeds of their various forces: the logistic support for the mechanized forces was very much faster than that for the infantry, the latter slowed by the plodding speed at which the huge number

ABOVE LEFT: *Soviet prisoners are marched into German captivity. Few of them survived the treatment they received in Germany.*

LEFT: *A German soldier searches a Soviet prisoner.*

OPPOSITE: *A scene typical of the German advance into the USSR during the summer of 1941, with PzKpfw III medium tanks waiting to push forward as soon as the fires had subsided in a burning Soviet village.*

of horses could bring up food, ammunition and other vital supplies. The problem was partially solved by allowing the armored forces to press on as spearheads, leaving the infantry to mop up, but the determination of the Soviet pockets further delayed the infantry, leading to dissension in the German camp as the gaps between the armor and the infantry lengthened. Convinced of the all-important factor of speed, the Panzer commanders wished to press on regardless of the infantry, but the army group commanders, almost all of them infantry, artillery, cavalry, and engineer officers by training, often tried to prevent this from happening. Inevitably, the marching infantry's lack of speed slowed the rate of overall advance, although it was still very rapid by the standards of the time.

Understandably, the Soviets were in total disarray. Had it not been for the extraordinary perseverance of the mass of Soviet soldiers and the implacable resolution of the Soviet dictator, Iosef Stalin, it is conceivable that the Soviet armed forces might have been dissolved. But these two factors just about held the Soviet armies together. Appalling as the losses were, Stalin was prepared to sacrifice almost any number of men to slow the German advance, for he appreciated the overriding need to dismantle the USSR's most important industrial facilities along the Germans' axes of advance, removing them to new sites beyond the Ural mountains. It is impossible to give a succinct idea of the efforts made by the Soviet men and women, from the very young to the ancient, to save the industrial plant on which, ultimately, the survival of their nation depended. Yet most of it was saved, and that which proved impossible to remove was destroyed to prevent it from falling into enemy hands. It was a national effort which ultimately saved the USSR, with lives being sacrificed in their hundreds of thousands to accomplish this task. Faced with the possible destruction of his country and his political philosophy, Stalin displayed no element of humanity at this time: commanders were shot or replaced wholesale, and losses were deemed

acceptable being the price of slowing the German advance.

Although Stalin was successful in this, the German progress was nonetheless remarkable, especially that of Army Group Center, with its two Panzergruppen. By the middle of July the 2nd and 3rd Panzergruppen had closed the trapdoor on a huge Soviet pocket to the west of Minsk, and once the slower forces had arrived to seal it off, the armor was then able to advance once more. But the Soviet losses in this early stage of the campaign were so great as to be almost incomprehensible: at Minsk, for example, the Soviets lost around 330,000 men, 2,500 tanks, and 1,500 pieces of artillery, although there is still no complete agreement as to the accuracy of these numbers. By August 5 Army Group Center, again in the form of its two Panzergruppen, had trapped 310,000 Soviets, 3,200 tanks, and 3,000 pieces of artillery at Smolensk. Army Group Center was thus only some 200 miles (320km) west of Moscow by this time, with virtually nothing to block its advance. Although making adequate progress to its north and south, Army

Groups North and South were facing problems not experienced by Army Group Center, being opposed by high-quality Soviet forces in a vast and difficult terrain, while Army Group South was suffering from a lack of adequate armored forces for the task in hand. For as the German forces advanced to the east, the 2,000-mile (3200-km) front on which they had started out was gradually widening, leaving the Germans with little alternative but to thin the troops at the front so as to be able to cover it completely. At the same time, the great length of the advance made supply increasingly difficult, especially as men, machines, and horses were becoming rapidly exhausted by the heat and dust of the Soviet summer, and by the very distances involved. Inevitably, the lack of depth in the German army, whose rapid expansion had emphasized the creation of "tooth" at the expense of "tail" elements, began to exert a major effect.

At this time Hitler stepped in, and the lack of proper strategic planning immediately became clear: the 2nd Panzergruppe and the 2nd Army were

detached to aid Army Group South, while the 3rd Panzergruppe was similarly detached to aid Army Group North. Although the short-term results of this alteration in emphasis helped the two flanking armies to catch up with Army Group Center, the long-term result was that the central force missed its one real chance of taking Moscow easily and in good time.

In the south, by August 21, the German forces had almost reached Kiev, the main city of Ukraine. With the aid of Guderian's armor coming down from the north past the eastern side of the Pripyet marshes, Kiev was now turned into an enormous pocket. When the city finally fell on September 20, some 665,000 Soviet troops fell with it in the pocket just to the east. While this was happening, General Erich von Manstein's 11th Army had been making good progress down the Yuzhni Bug river toward Crimea.

In the north, Hoth's forces had also enabled Army Group North to speed its advance, and real progress was being made in the direction of Leningrad. Although much of the momentum of the early days had been lost, October found the Germans handily placed: von Leeb was able to take Leningrad under siege in October, von Bock was still pushing on from Smolensk with his infantry, and von Rundstedt reached the Don river on October 15, posing a threat to the major industrial cities of Kharkov and Rostov. Only in the Finnish theater was progress slower and more limited. The Finns were content just to retake the portions of Finland lost in the "Winter War," and von Falkenhorst's army in the far north was bogged down in very difficult terrain far short of its target.

In the air, the Luftwaffe continued to dominate, having destroyed more than 4,500 first-line Soviet aircraft for the loss of less than 2,000 of its own machines. But in the rear areas the problems of the Germans were increasing: units which could have been used to good effect at the front now had to be detached to guard the lines of communication against the growing threat of Soviet partisan groups. But worst of all, the weather was beginning to break. The fall rains had begun, turning the unmetaled Russian roads to mud and further hampering the German advance in a foretaste of the freezing winter that was still to come. The Germans were running out of time, and the delay occasioned by the Balkan excursion of April was now having its effect.

Now Hitler changed his mind once more. Moscow once again became the primary objective, and von Bock was given back the land and air forces lent to von Leeb and von Rundstedt. Army Group Center was thus able to accelerate its progress, and between September 30 and October 7 created yet another great Soviet pocket, this time just to the west of Vyazma, where the haul was more than 650,000 men. A

ABOVE: *The crew of a German 0.79-inch (20-mm cannon) wait for a target of opportunity as German infantry push forward around it.*

little under a fortnight later, the leading elements of Army Group Center reached Mozhaisk, only 40 miles (65km) from Moscow. On the map, the German position seemed to be good, but at the front it was rather poor, for all formations were down to less than 50 percent strength in men and machines, and the change in the weather had caught the Germans totally unprepared. As it was expected that the campaign would be over before the arrival of winter, no preparation had been made to provide the troops with winter combat clothing. Moreover, at the beginning of November, front-line German formations had begun to detect the arrival of fresh Soviet reserves, just at the time when they themselves were approaching the limits of their endurance. At the same time, the Soviets had reorganized their command structure. Budenny had been replaced as commander-in-chief of the South-West Front by Timoshenko, whose place as head of the West Front had been taken by the greatest soldier the USSR was to produce in World War II, General Georgi Zhukov. Under Zhukov's driving force, the defenses before Moscow were strengthened, and try as they might during November and December, the Germans were unable to break through, leading to desperate fighting in appalling winter conditions.

Timoshenko's arrival in the south strengthened the Soviet resistance there, and on November 15 the Germans were driven out of Rostov-na-Donu, where the Don river debouches into the Sea of Azov, in this, the first major German reverse of the Soviet campaign. The German command structure was also altered at this time: by December 5 Field-Marshal Walther von Reichenau had replaced von Rundstedt, and Field-Marshal Günther-Hans von Kluge had succeeded von Bock. By this date the temperature had fallen far below freezing point, the only winter clothing available being that which had been stripped from the Soviet dead and prisoners; the German armies had reached the limit of their endurance, with the result that they paused, exhausted, a mere 25 miles (40km) from Moscow.

Then the Soviets struck back. Fresh troops, arriving from Siberia and thus used to the cold and equipped for it, were carefully marshaled by Zhukov and unleashed in a great counteroffensive around Moscow. The German generals called for a strategic retreat in the face of this Soviet attack, but Hitler absolutely forbade any such move. Quite extraordinarily, the Germans were able to hold their position at a moment when any withdrawal might have turned into a rout. Up to the end of the year, the great Soviet offensives around Moscow, and near Izyum in Crimea, slowly drove the Germans back, finally dashing any hopes of defeating the USSR in one devastating round. Hitler's decision to hold Moscow was typical of the German dictator, and within the context of the battle for it was a brilliant piece of insight. Unfortunately for the Germans, however, it further reinforced Hitler's high opinion of himself as a military genius, and also served to convince him of the basic correctness of holding ground regardless of the cost in men and matériel. This latter conviction was to cause the German army enormous and needless losses in the years to come in what was known to the Soviets as the "Great Patriotic War" and to the western world as the Eastern Front of World War II.

The final results of the campaign infuriated Hitler, and he completely reshuffled his high command to make himself the actual as well as titular head of the German armed forces. Field-Marshal Walther von Brauchitsch lost his job as commander-in-chief of the army, and Hitler also took over as head both of the Oberkommando des Heeres (OKH, or army high command), with General Franz Halder as its chief of staff, and of the Oberkommando der Wehrmacht (OKW, or armed forces high command), with Field-Marshal Wilhelm Keitel as its chief of staff. The OKH ran the war on the Eastern Front and the OKW that on other fronts. Among other field commanders replaced were von Leeb and Höpner. Although they failed, and their failures cost them the war, the Germans had performed a prodigious feat in purely military terms. But so too had the Soviets. The Germans had lost some 800,000 men, most of them difficult to replace veterans, while the Soviets had suffered some 1.5 million men killed and somewhat more than 2 million taken prisoner, as well as millions of civilian dead. Yet in the long term, Stalin's policy proved strategically sound, in that it saved the USSR's most important war-making industries.

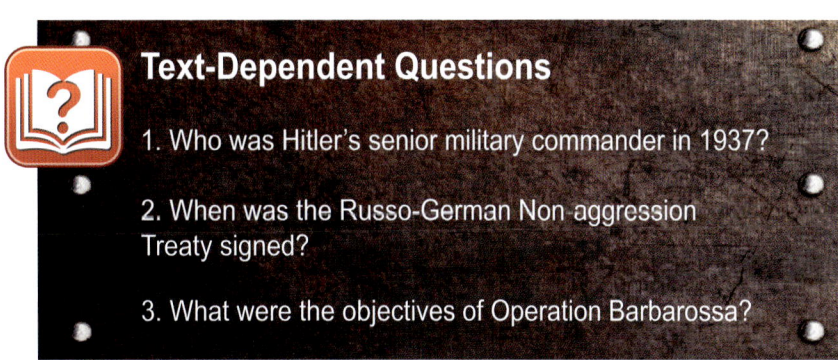

Text-Dependent Questions

1. Who was Hitler's senior military commander in 1937?

2. When was the Russo-German Non-aggression Treaty signed?

3. What were the objectives of Operation Barbarossa?

Research Projects

Why did Operation Barbarossa fail?

WORLD WAR II

Chapter Eight
THE BATTLE OF THE ATLANTIC
1940–1941

As the threat of a German invasion of southern England receded, the Royal Navy was able to concentrate once more on the problem of the Atlantic convoys. In September 1940, the USA made an important declaration of sympathy by exchanging 50 old destroyers in exchange for a 99-year lease of British bases around the world. These destroyers were fit only for second-line duties, but made it possible for newer destroyers to be released for fleet work; many of the old 'four-stack' destroyers were still in service at the end of the war.

Coastal escorts and air patrols proved moderately successful against the U-boats, so forcing them to venture into the Western Approaches in search of targets. Here the new U-boat bases in the Bay of Biscay gave the Germans an important advantage, and the British were hard-pressed to extend cover to convoys deeper in the Atlantic. But Iceland had been occupied in July 1940 by British and Canadian troops to prevent a possible German occupation, and the island provided airfields and a refuelling base which partly offset the U-boats' advantage.

Throughout 1941 the USA was benevolent in its neutrality, for President Franklin D. Roosevelt knew that U.S. interests would not benefit from a German victory over the UK. In March 1941, the Lend-Lease Act was enacted, allowing more ships and equipment to be provided. In April the USA declared that its defence zone, in which U.S. merchant ships were escorted by U.S. Navy warships, would be extended to 26° West, regardless of whether they were carrying war matériel to the UK or not.

The worst problem for many convoy escorts was their lack of endurance. Destroyers were designed for high-speed

The Start of World War II: The Flood of the German Tide

sensors required. Unfortunately, none was ready until early in 1942, but existing escorts were given as much new equipment as possible to help them fight back in the meantime. In May 1941, the first surface warning radar set went to sea in a corvette. Although the Asdic detection device was very effective in locating submerged U-boats, it had a weakness in that contact was lost during the final stages of a depth-charge attack. To remedy this, a new ahead-firing weapon had to be developed, which promised to increase the rate of 'kills'. The resulting Hedgehog was a multiple spigot mortar, firing small contact-fused bombs in a pattern, the first ship being equipped with it by the end of 1941.

All these countermeasures were needed as a matter of the greatest urgency, for 1941 was a critical year, with shipping losses increasing rapidly and ever-increasing numbers of U-boats coming into service. From a total of 755,000 tons in 1939, shipping losses rose to 3.991 million tons, or 1,000 ships, in 1940. And despite rising output from the shipyards and ever-increasing skill in anti-submarine tactics, the total rose to 1,300 ships, or 4.328 million tons, in 1941. Losses at this rate were unsustainable over the long term, and in August 1941, at the 'Atlantic Charter' meeting, the USA agreed that its warships would henceforward be permitted to escort all merchant ships irrespective of nationality, while Canadian warships would similarly be allowed to escort U.S. ships. The U.S. Navy was already handing over its

attack, with slender hulls unsuited to North Atlantic weather, and their turbines were not economical. Many of the older destroyers were turned into long-range escorts by replacing one of the boilers with additional bunkerage, and the first of these was taken in hand in January 1941. The corvettes, which were now coming into service in large numbers from British and Canadian shipyards, had good endurance but lacked speed. This was inevitable, for the design had been framed to make the best use of available machinery, but by 1941 U-boats had taken to attacking convoys on the surface at night, and at top speed were capable of out-distancing a corvette. Another problem was that convoy work demanded a great deal of loitering to investigate a suspected underwater contact, or high-speed dashes to find stragglers before herding them back to the convoy.

The answer was the creation of a fully optimized North Atlantic escort, possessing both long endurance and moderately high speed and carrying all the weapons and sensors needed for the anti-submarine task. The answer to the need was the 'River'-class frigate, which had twice the power of the corvette and ample space for the weapons and

escorted ships to Anglo-Canadian escorts at a predetermined Mid-Ocean Meeting Point, but in August 1941 this so-called 'Chop Line' was moved to 22° 58' West to relieve the strain on British escorts.

While all this was happening on the convoy routes, the German navy was planning a bold stroke. The battleship *Bismarck* was ready for sea in the spring of 1941, in the hope that it would be sent into the Atlantic with the heavy cruiser *Prinz Eugen*, to attack convoys which could disrupt the whole delicate organization, even for a short time, and allow the U-boats to slaughter unescorted ships. A further aim was to effect a junction with the battle-cruisers *Scharnhorst* and *Gneisenau*, which were at Brest. The prospect of three Nazi capital ships at large in the Atlantic appalled the British, who were therefore prepared to do anything to prevent the break-out of the *Bismarck*.

On May 26 1941 the *Bismarck* and *Prinz Eugen* sailed from Bergen, heading for the Denmark Strait between Greenland and Iceland on their way to the Atlantic shipping routes. Their departure was reported to the Admiralty and two days later they were sighted by a pair of British cruisers patrolling in the Denmark Strait. The old British battle-cruiser *Hood*, and the new battleship, *Prince of Wales*, had been in Iceland, so they were able to intercept the German ships on the morning of the following day. The British seemed about to frustrate the German plans, but then the *Hood* blew up after firing only three salvoes, apparently as a result of a fire caused by a German shell. Although the *Prince of Wales* was only slightly damaged it was so new that half its guns were not firing, and the admiral commanding the cruisers ordered her captain to break off the action. For two days the whereabouts of the German ships was unknown, but eventually massive air and sea searches located the *Bismarck*, the *Prinz Eugen* having already been detached to Brest. The aircraft carrier *Ark Royal* was able to launch a torpedo-bomber strike, and two torpedoes damaged the battleship's

The Start of World War II: The Flood of the German Tide

steering gear; by nightfall on May 26 Vice-Admiral Günther Lütjens knew that his ship was doomed.

On the following morning the Home Fleet battleships *Rodney* and *King George V* approached the *Bismarck* and opened fire at the modest range of 16,000 yards (14630m). This time the *Bismarck*'s gunnery was wild and the German ship failed to score a hit on either ship, apart from a single medium-calibre shell which failed to detonate. Under a hail of fire the *Bismarck* rapidly

OPPOSITE ABOVE: *The German battleship, Bismarck, is caught by the camera in the North Sea during 1941. This great ship was hunted down and sunk in May of that year in the North Atlantic.*

OPPOSITE BELOW: *The battleship King George V was one of Britain's capital ships involved in the search for the Bismarck during May 1941.*

ABOVE: *Admiral Karl Dönitz played a major role in the naval history of World War II.*

ABOVE RIGHT: *Fairey Swordfish torpedo bombers on the flight deck of the British aircraft carrier Victorious. The ship was commissioned in May 1941, serving with distinction until well beyond the end of World War II.*

became a flaming hulk, and her guns were silent in half an hour. The ship lay so low in the water that the British shells were having no real effect, and after another hour of gunfire the British commander, Admiral Sir John Tovey, ordered the cruiser *Dorsetshire* to sink the *Bismarck* with torpedoes. The *Bismarck*'s career had lasted for three days, and there were but 110 survivors.

The Germans had placed too much faith in the *Bismarck*'s ability to withstand attack. The ship should have returned to Germany after the damage suffered to its fuel tanks, caused by the *Prince of Wales*, and might well have eluded the Home Fleet in the poor visibility that prevailed. Instead, Lütjens opted to continue the Atlantic sortie with what amounted to major battle damage, and was later forced to make for Brest for lack of fuel. The German navy had often been accused of tactical timidity, but on this occasion it showed a degree of foolhardiness that is difficult to understand.

With the destruction of the *Bismarck*, the German navy virtually abandoned all idea of using its surface fleet aggressively. Certainly it was never the same threat to the Atlantic convoys again, Hitler admitting as much early the following year when

he ordered the *Scharnhorst*, *Gneisenau* and *Prinz Eugen* back to Germany. The *Bismarck*'s sister ship, the *Tirpitz*, was completed late in 1941, but also spent a largely inactive career in Norwegian waters, content to tie down British ships by the mere threat of its presence rather than by making any determined attack.

By the end of 1941 the Battle of the Atlantic had become nothing more than a grim struggle of attrition. The entry of the USA into the war was only a matter of time, but Admiral Karl Dönitz tried to keep his U-boats from precipitating hostilities. Between September and December 1941 a series of incidents, including the torpedoing of three American destroyers off Iceland, strained relations to breaking point, but still the spirit of isolationism was strong enough to keep the USA from declaring war on Germany. In December 1941 the impasse was finally resolved by the Japanese attack on Pearl Harbor, followed by Hitler's monumentally foolish and unnecessary declaration of war on the USA. The American entry into the war marked the end of the first phase of the Battle of the Atlantic, though in fact its grimmest part was yet to com

TIME LINE OF WORLD WAR II

1939
Germany invades Poland on September 1.

Two days later Britain and France declare war on Germany.

1940
Rationing starts in the UK.

German "Blitzkrieg" overwhelms and overpowers Belgium, Holland, and France.

Churchill becomes Prime Minister of Britain.

British Expeditionary Force evacuated from Dunkirk.

Britain is victorious in the Battle of Britain. Hitler to postpones invasion plans.

1941
Operation Barbarossa commences – the invasion of Russia begins.

The Blitz continues against Britain. Major cities are badly damaged.

Allies take Tobruk in North Africa, and resist German attacks.

Japan attacks Pearl Harbor, and the U.S. enters the war.

1942
Germany suffers setbacks at Stalingrad and El Alamein.

Singapore falls to the Japanese in February – around 25,000 prisoners taken.

American naval victory at Battle of Midway, in June, marks turning point in Pacific War.

Mass murder of Jewish people at Auschwitz begins.

1943
Germany surrenders at Stalingrad. Germany's first major defeat.

The Allies are victorious in North Africa The invasion of Italy is launched.

Italy surrenders to the Allies, but Germany takes over the fight.

British and Indian forces fight Japanese in Burma.

1944
Allies land at Anzio and bomb monastery at Monte Cassino.

Soviet offensive gathers pace in Eastern Europe.

D-Day: The Allied invasion of France. Paris is liberated in August.

Guam liberated by the U.S. *Okinawa*, and Iwo Jima bombed.

1945
Auschwitz liberated by Soviet troops. Russians reach Berlin. Hitler commits suicide and Germany surrenders on May 7.

Truman becomes President of the U.S. on Roosevelt's death.

Attlee replaces Churchill.

After atomic bombs are dropped on Hiroshima and Nagasaki, Japan surrenders on August 14.

OPPOSITE: *American tank in Carentan, Normandy, France. 1944.*

The Start of World War II: The Flood of the German Tide

Series Glossary of Key Terms

Allied Powers A coalition of nations that fought against the Axis powers.

ANZAC An Australian or New Zealand soldier.

Appeasement A policy of agreeing to hostile demands in order to maintain peace.

Aryan In Nazi ideology, a Caucasian especially of Nordic type.

Auschwitz An industrial town in Poland and site of Nazi concentration camp during World War II.

Axis Powers An alignment of nations that fought against the Allied forces in World War II.

Blitzkrieg A surprise and violent offensive by air and ground forces.

Concentration camp A camp where prisoners of war are detained or confined.

D-Day June 6, 1944. The Allied invasion of France in World War II began.

Fascism A political movement or philosophy that exalts nation and race above the individual with an autocratic government and a dictator as leader.

Führer A leader or tyrant.

Final Solution The Nazi program to exterminate all the Jews throughout Europe.

Gestapo A secret-police employing devious ways of controlling people considered disloyal.

Holocaust The mass slaughter of European civilians especially the Jews by the Nazis during World War II.

Kamikaze A Japanese pilot trained to make suicidal crash attacks upon ships in World War II.

Lebensraum Territory considered necessary by Nazis for national existence.

Luftwaffe German air force.

Maginot Line Defensive fortifications on the eastern border of France during World War II.

Manhattan Project The code name for the secret U.S. project set up in 1942 to develop an atomic bomb.

Nazi An advocate of policies characteristic of Nazism.

Pact of Steel A military alliance between Nazi Germany and Fascist Italy concluded on May 22, 1939.

Panzer A German tank.

Potsdam Conference A conference held in Potsdam in the summer of 1945 where Roosevelt, Stalin, and Churchill drew up plans for the adminstration of Germany and Poland after World War II ended.

U-boat A German submarine especially in World War I and II.

The Versailles Treaty The treaty imposed on Germany by the Alllied powers in 1920 after the end of World War I.

Yalta Conference A conference held in Yalta in February 1945, where Roosevelt, Stalin, and Churchill planned the finals statge of World War II and agreed to new boundaries and territorial division in Europe.

Further Reading and Internet Resources

WEBSITES

http://www.bbc.co.uk/history/worldwars/wwtwo

http://www.history.com/topics/world-war-ii

https://www.britannica.com/event/World-War-II

http://www.world-war-2.info/

BOOKS

Hourly History. *World War II The Definitive Visual Guide.* Oxford University Press, 2010

Richard Overy. *The New York Times Complete World War II: The Coverage of the Entire Conflict.* 2016

Smithsonian. *World War II The Definitive Visual Guide* DK Publishing Inc., 2015.

If you enjoyed this book take a look at Mason Crest's other war series:

The Civil War, The Vietnam War, Major U.S. Historical Wars.

Index

In this book, page numbers in ***bold italic font*** indicate photos or videos.

A

Admiral Graf Spee, 41, *42*
Africa. *See* North Africa
air force
    British, 33, 35–39, *36*, *38–39*, 42, 45, 50, 57
    German, 12, *12*, 15–16, 22, 23, *25*, 29–30, 31, 33, 34, *35*, 35–39, *37–39*, 49, *56*, 56–58, 64, 66
    Italian, 44, 47, *47*
    Polish, 14, 15
    Soviet, 18, 64
Allies
    Battle of Britain with, 35–39, *35–39*, 61–62
    naval war 1939-1940 with, 40–43, *40–43*
    North Africa battles of, 44–53, *44–53*
    Scandinavian support from, 21–27
    Western European battles of, 28–39, *28–39*, 40–43, *40–43*
    Yugoslavia and Greece invasion response of, 54–59
    See also specific countries
Atlantic Charter, 69
Auchinleck, Claude, 25, 51, 53
Australia, WW II involvement of, 46–47, 48, 50, 54, 57
Austria, German annexation of, 12
Axis powers, 34
    See also specific countries; Tripartite Pact

B

Baillie-Grohman, H. T., 56
Battle of the Atlantic, 43, 68–71, *68–71*
Battle of Britain, 35–39, *35–39*, 61–62
Battle of the Bzura, 16–17
Battle of the River Plate, 41, *42*
Belgium, German invasion of, 28–29, 30–31, 33

Beresford-Peirse, N. M. de la P., 44, 50
Bergonzoli, Annibale, 46
Berti, Mario, 44
Béthouart, Marie Émile, 25–27
Billotte, Gaston, 28, 32
Bismarck, 70, 70–71
Blaskowitz, Johannes, 15
Brand, Quintin, 36
Budenny, Semyon, 63, 67
Bulgaria, WW II involvement of, 54, *54*, 55, 56

C

Canada, WW II involvement of, 40, 43, 68, 69–70
Carton de Wiart, A., 23, 25
casualties
    British, 27, 39, 42, 46, 51, 53, 59
    Finnish, 21
    French, 27
    German, 27, 33, 39, 53, 59, 67
    Norwegian, 27
    Polish, 27
    Soviet, 20, 21, 65, 66, 67
Chamberlain, Neville, *28*
Churchill, Winston, 33
Combe, J. F. B., 48
Cora, André, 28
Creagh, M. O'Moore, 44, 48
Cunningham, Alan, 51–53
Cunningham, Andrew, 58
Czechoslovakia, German occupation of, 12–13

D

de Gaulle, Charles, 33, 34
Denmark, German seizure of, 21–22, *26*
Dietl, Eduard, 25–26
Dill, John, 54
Dönitz, Karl, 40, 71
Dowding, Hugh, 35, 38
Dunkirk evacuation, 33, 42

E

Eden, Anthony, 54
Enigma cipher machine, *6*
Essemann, Frederik Christian, *26*

F

Finland
    Soviet attack on, *8*, 18–21, *18–21*
    Soviet invasion role of, 62–63, 66
France
    declaration of war by, 14
    German invasion of, 28–34, *29–34*, 42–43
    lack of opposition by, 12–13
    navy of, 40, 42, 43
    refugees from, *34*
    Scandinavian support from, 23, 25–27
Frank, Hans, *17*
Freyberg, Bernard, *56*, 57, 59

G

Gamelin, Maurice, 28, 32
Germany
    air force of, 12, *12*, 15–16, 22, 23, *25*, 29–30, 31, 33, 34, *35*, 35–39, *37–39*, 49, *56*, 56–58, 64, 66
    Austria annexation by, 12
    Battle of the Atlantic with, 43, 68–71, *68–71*
    Battle of Britain with, 35–39, *35–39*, 61–62
    Belgium invasion by, 28–29, 30–31, 33
    Czechoslovakia occupation by, 12–13
    Finland not supported by, *19*, 20
    France invasion by, 28–34, *29–34*, 42–43
    Luxembourg invasion by, 30–31
    navy of, 21, 22, *23*, *24*, *25*, 27, 35, 40–43, *40–43*, 68–71, *70*
    Netherlands invasion by, 28, 29–30
    North Africa invasion by, 48–53, *49–53*
    Norway and Denmark seizure by, 21–27, *22–27*, 42–43
    Poland defeated by, 12–17, *12–17*

76

Russo-German non-aggression treaty with, 14, *19,* 61
Soviet Union invasion by, *27, 60–66,* 60–67
Tripartite Pact with, 34, 54, 55
Yugoslavia and Greece seizure by, 54–59, *54–59,* 62, 64
Giraud, Henri, 28
Godwin-Austen, A. R., 51
Göring, Hermann, 33, *34,* 35
Gort, General Lord, 28, 33
Gott, W. H. E., 50
Graziani, Rodolfo, 44–45, 47
Greece, German seizure of, 54–59, *54–59,* 62, 64
Guderian, Heinz, *6, 15,* 17, 29, 30, 31, 32, 33, 62, 66

H
Hagglund, J. Woldemar, 18
Halder, Franz, 67
Hitler, Adolf
   Battle of the Atlantic under, 71
   Battle of Britain under, 35, 37, 39
   "Europe together against Bolshevism" speech by, *62*
   France and Western Europe invasion under, 30, *32,* 33
   naval war 1939-1940 under, 40–41, 42–43
   North Africa invasion under, 48
   Poland and Eastern Europe defeat under, 12–17, *15*
   Soviet Union invasion under, 60–62, 64–67
   Yugoslavia and Greece seizure under, 54, 55, 57, 59
Höpner, Erich, 62, 67
Hoth, Hermann, 29, 31, 62, 66
Hungary, WW II involvement of, 55, 62

I
Iceland, Allied occupation of, 68
India, North Africa battles involving, 44, 46, 48, 50, 51
Italy
   France attacks by, 34
   Greece invasion by, 54
   North Africa invasion by, 44–49, *45, 47–48,* 50, *51,* 51–52
   Tripartite Pact with, 34
   Yugoslavia and Greece invasion role of, 55
Iwo Jima Memorial, *10,* 11

J
Japan, Tripartite Pact with, 34

K
Keitel, Wilhelm, 67
Kesselring, Albert, 15, 35
King George V, 70, 71
Kummetz, Oskar, 22
Kutrzeba, General, 16
Kuznetsov, F. I., 63

L
Langsdorff, Hans, 41, *42*
Lebensraum, 13, 60
Leigh-Mallory, Trafford, 36
List, Wilhelm, 15, *32, 54,* 56
Lithuania, Soviet annexation of, 17
Löhr, Alexander, 15
Luftwaffe. *See* air force: German
Lütjens, Günther, 70
Luxembourg, German invasion of, 30–31

M
Mackay, I. G., 46
Mackesy, P. J., 22–23
Maginot Line, 28, *31,* 34
Mannerheim, Carl Gustaf von, 18–21, *19,* 63
Marine Corps Iwo Jima Memorial, *10,* 11
Meindl, Eugen, 59
Mihailovic, Draza-Dragoljub, 56
Mölders, Werner, *34*
Molotov cocktails, *18,* 20, *21*
Morgan, H. de R., 23, 25
Morshead, L. J., 50
Mussolini, Benito, 34, 44, *45,* 54

N
National World War II Memorial *10,* 11
navy
   Battle of the Atlantic, 43, 68–71, *68–71*
   British, 21, 22, *26,* 27, 35, 40–43, *43,* 45, 50, 57, 58–59, 68–71, *68–71*
   Canadian, 69–70
   French, 40, 42, 43
   German, 21, 22, *23, 24, 25,* 27, 35, 40–43, *40–43,* 68–71, *70*
   Greek, *58*
   naval war 1939-1940, 40–43, *40–43*
   US, 68, 69–70
Nazi Party, rise of, 12
Neame, P., 44
Netherlands, German invasion of, 28, 29–30
New Zealand, WW II involvement of, 51, 54, *56,* 57
Norrie, C. W. M., 51
North Africa
   German invasion of, 48–53, *49–53*
   Italian invasion of, 44–49, *45, 47–48,* 50, *51,* 51–52
Norway
   German seizure of, 21–27, *22–27,* 42–43
   Soviet invasion role of, 63

O
O'Connor, Richard, 44, 46–47, 48, 50
Operation Barbarossa, *60–66,* 60–67
Operation Battleaxe, 50
Operation Brevity, 50
Operation Compass, 46
Operation Crusader, 51–53
Operation Merkur, 57
Ostermann, Hugo, 18

P

Paget, B. T. C., 25
Panzers. *See* tanks: German
Papagos, Alexandros, 56
Paris, Germans in, *32,* 34
Park, Keith, 36
Pétain, Henri, 34
Poland
    Battle of the Bzura in, 16–17
    German defeat of, 12–17, *12–17*
    Scandinavian support from, 25–26, 27
    Soviet occupation of, 17, 61
Prien, Günther, *41*
prisoners of war
    British, *24,* 50
    German, 36, *39,* 50
    Italian, 46, 48
    Polish, 17
    Soviet, *64*

Q

Quislin, Vidkun, 21

R

radar, 36, *36,* 37, 69
Raeder, Erich, *43*
Ramsey, Bertram, 33
Reinhardt, Georg-Hans, 29, 31, 33
Reynaud, Paul, 34
Ribbentrop, Joachim, 60
Ringel, Julius, 59
Ritchie, N. M., 53
Romania, WW II involvement of, 17, 62
Rommel, Erwin, *29,* 30, 31, 32, 33, 48–51, *49,* 52–53
Roosevelt, Franklin D., 68
Royal Air Force. *See* air force: British
Royal Navy. *See* air force: British
Ruge, Otto, 23, 27
Russo-Finnish Treaty, 21
Russo-German non-aggression treaty, 14, *19,* 61
Rydz-Smigly, Edward, 14, 16

S

Saul, Richard, 36
Scandinavian conflicts, 18–27
    See also Denmark; Finland; Iceland; Norway; Sweden
Scobie, R. M., 52
Selby, A. R., 46
Siilasvuo, Hjalmar, 20
Simovic, Dusan, 55
Smuts, Jan, *49*
sonar, 43
South Africa, North Africa battles involving, *49,* 51
Soviet Union
    Finland attacked by, *8,* 18–21, *18–21*
    German agreements/treaties with, 12, 14, 17, *19,* 61
    German invasion of, *27, 60–66,* 60–67
    Lithuania annexation by, 17
    Poland occupation by, 17, 61
Sperrie, Hugo, 35
Stalin, Josef
    Finland attacked under, 18, 20
    German invasion response of, *61,* 63, 65, 67
Student, Kurt, 57–59
Stumpff, Hans-Jürgen, 35
submarines
    British, 42
    German, 40, *41,* 42, 43, 68–71
Sweden, German iron from, 21, *27*

T

Talvela, Paavo, 20
tanks
    British, *3,* 33, 44, *45,* 45–47, *46,* 50–52, *53,* 54
    French, 29, *29,* 33
    German, 15, *16,* 16–17, *22,* 29, *29, 30,* 30–33, *33,* 34, 48, 50–53, *51,* 55–56, *61,* 62, 64–66, *65*
    Italian, 44, *45,* 50, 51–52
    Soviet, 18, 20, 21, *21,* 64

US, *73*
timeline of World War II, 72
Timoshenko, Semyon, 20, 21, 63, 67
Tovey, John, 71
treaties
    Polish-German non-aggression treaty, 13
    Russo-Finnish Treaty, 21
    Russo-German non-aggression treaty, 14, *19,* 61
    Treaty of Delimitation and Friendship, 17
    Treaty of Versailles, 12
Tripartite Pact, 34, 54, 55
Tuompo, Vilpo, 18

U

U-boats. *See* submarines: German
United Kingdom
    air force of, 33, 35–39, *36, 38–39,* 42, 45, 50, 57
    Battle of the Atlantic with, 43, 68–71, *68–71*
    Battle of Britain with, 35–39, *35–39,* 61–62
    British Expeditionary Force of, 28, 30, 32, 33
    declaration of war by, 14
    Iceland occupation by, 68
    lack of opposition by, 12–13
    navy of, 21, 22, *26,* 27, 35, 40–43, *43,* 45, 50, 57, 58–59, 68–71, *68–71*
    North Africa battles involving, *44–46,* 44–53, *50, 53*
    radar of, 36, *36,* 37, 69
    Scandinavian support from, 21–27
    sonar of, 43
    troops entering Germany, *2*
    Western Europe battles involving, 28, *28,* 30–33, 40–43, *42–43*
    Yugoslavia and Greece invasion response of, 54–59
United States
    Battle of the Atlantic response of, 68, 69–70

declaration of war by, 71
Marine Corps Iwo Jima Memorial of, *10,* 11
navy of, 68, 69–70
soliders in France, *5*
UK supplies from, 40, 43, 68
USSR. *See* Soviet Union

V
Victorious, 71
von Bock, Fedor, 15, 29, 30, 32, 62, 66, 67
von Brauchitsch, Walther, 67
von Falkenhorst, Nikolaus, 21, 63, 66
von Kleist, Paul Ludwig Ewald, 32, 33, 55, 62
von Kluge, Günther-Hans, 15, 29, 67
von Küchler, Georg, 15, 30
von Leeb, Wilhelm Ritter, 29, 62, 66, 67
von Manstein, Erich, 29, 66
von Reichenau, Walther, 15, 30, 67
von Richthofen, Wolfram, 57
von Rundstedt, Karl Rudolf Gerd, 15, *15,* 29, 32, 33, 62, 66, 67
von Seeckt, Hans, 12
von Werra, Franz, *39*
von Wietersheim, Gustav, 29
Voroshilov, Klimenti, 63

W
Wallenius, Kurt, 18
Warburton-Lee, B. A. W., 22
Wavell, Archibald, 44, *44,* 45–46, 48, 50–51
weapons and artillery
 British, 42
 Finnish, *18,* 20, 21, *21*
 French, 30, 34
 German, *19,* 42, *49,* 50, *66*
 Greek, 57
 Italian, 44, 45–47, *47, 51*
 Polish, *12, 13, 14*
 Soviet, 21, 64
 See also tanks
Weygand, Maxime, 32–34
Wilson, Henry Maitland, 54, 55, 56

Winter War, *8,* 18–21, *18–21*
women, as Finnish auxiliaries, *20*

Y
Yugoslavia, German seizure of, 54–59, *54– 59,* 62, 64

Z
Zhukov, Georgi, 67

PHOTOGRAPHIC ACKNOWLEDGEMENTS

All images in this book are supplied by Cody Images and are in the public domain.

The contents of this book was first published as *WORLD WAR II*.

ABOUT THE AUTHOR
Christopher Chant

Christopher Chant is a successful writer on aviation and modern military matters, and has a substantial number of authoritative titles to his credit. He was born in Cheshire, England in December 1945, and spent his childhood in East Africa, where his father was an officer in the Colonial Service. He returned to the UK for his education at the King's School, Canterbury (1959–64) and at Oriel College, Oxford (1964–68).

Aviation in particular and military matters in general have long been a passion, and after taking his degree he moved to London as an assistant editor on the Purnell partworks, *History of the Second World War* (1968–69) and *History of the First World War* (1969–72). On completion of the latter he moved to Orbis Publishing as editor of the partwork, *World War II* (1972–74), on completion of which he decided to become a freelance writer and editor.

Living first in London, then in Lincolnshire after his marriage in 1978, and currently in Sutherland, at the north-western tip of Scotland, he has also contributed as editor and writer to the partworks, *The Illustrated Encyclopedia of Aircraft*, *War Machine*, *Warplane*, *Take-Off*, *World Aircraft Information Files* and *World Weapons*, and to the magazine *World Air Power Journal*. In more recent years he was also involved in the creation of a five-disk CR-ROM series, covering the majority of the world's military aircraft from World War I to the present, and also in the writing of scripts for a number of video cassette and TV programs, latterly for Continuo Creative.

As sole author, Chris has more than 90 books to his credit, many of them produced in multiple editions and co-editions, including more than 50 on aviation subjects. As co-author he has contributed to 15 books, ten of which are also connected with aviation. He has written the historical narrative and technical database for a five-disk *History of Warplanes* CD-ROM series, and has been responsible for numerous video cassette programs on military and aviation matters, writing scripts for several TV programmes and an A–Z 'All the World's Aircraft' section in Aerospace/Bright Star *World Aircraft Information Files* partwork. He has been contributing editor to a number of books on naval, military and aviation subjects as well as to numerous partworks concerned with military history and technology. He has also produced several continuity card sets on aircraft for publishers such as Agostini, Del Prado, Eaglemoss, Edito-Service and Osprey.